ScottForesman
In Charge 2

WORKBOOK

JUDITH E. MENDEL
ESL Consultant
Evanston, Illinois

ScottForesman

I would like to thank my family, friends, and my editors at ScottForesman for their support, insights, and encouragement. This book is dedicated to my family.
                                                                        Judith E. Mendel

Credits:

27: Edward Lear, THE COMPLETE NONSENSE BOOK, edited by Lady Strachey, 1912. New York: Dodd, Mead & Company. **30:** "The Panther" from VERSES FROM 1929 ON by Ogden Nash. Copyright 1940 by Ogden Nash. By permission of Little, Brown and Company. **57:** George S. Thommen, IS THIS YOUR DAY? New York: Crown Publishers, Inc., 1973, p. 128. **71:** The Editors of Time-Life Books, PLANET EARTH, VOLCANO. Alexandria, VA: Time-Life Books, p. 99. **77:** "Things my Mother Taught Me" by Steve Calechman. Reprinted by permission of Steve Calechman. **82:** Four bars of music and lyrics from AMERICA THE BEAUTIFUL by K. Bates and S. Ward. Copyright © 1987 by Studio 224 c/o CPP/BELWIN, INC., P.O. Box 4340, Miami, FL 33014. International Copyright Secured. Made in U.S.A. All Rights Reserved. **90:** From "Second Thoughts about Role Models" by Johnetta B. Cole. Appeared in McCall's, February 1991. Reprinted by permission of the author.

Unless otherwise acknowledged, all photographs are the property of ScottForesman. Page abbreviations are as follows: (T) top, (B) bottom, (L) left, (R) right, (C) center. **2:** COMSTOCK INC.; **4T, 4B:** Culver Pictures; **9:** D. Logan/H. Armstrong Roberts; **10:** AP/Wide World; **12:** Milt & Joan Mann/ Cameramann International, Ltd.; **13:** AP/Wide World; **29L:** Robert P. Carr; **29C:** Douglas Faulkner; **33L:** AP/Wide World; **33C:** AP/Wide World; **33R:** The Bettmann Archive; **35T:** UPI/Bettmann; **35B:** AP/Wide World; **42:** Hanna Barbera/Shooting Star; **43:** The Kobal Collection/SuperStock International; **58:** Christopher Brown/Stock Boston; **59:** Walter Hodges/ H. Armstrong Roberts; **66:** The Bettmann Archive; **67:** AP/Wide World; **69:** UPI/Bettmann; **70:** H. Armstrong Roberts; **73R:** Courtesy Harley Schwadron; **79L:** UPI/Bettmann; **79R:** Mark Twain Memorial, Hartford, CT; **81:** Anthro-Photo; **82T:** Papikyan/Novosti/SOVFOTO; **82B:** Robert Llewellyn/ Superstock; **84:** Milt & Joan Mann/Cameramann International, Ltd.; **87:** Four x Five/Superstock; **89:** Courtesy of Ravinia Festival; **92:** Courtesy The United Nations.

Illustrations by Paige Billin-Frye 26; Eldon Doty 3, 6, 77, 78, 91; Gioia Fiammenghi 13, 14, 20, 22; T.R. Garcia 11, 19, 53, 60; Brian Karas 49, 51; Kees de Kiefte 17, 18, 25; Joe Rogers 36, 65; Trudy Rogers 1, 57; Steven Schindler 30; George Ulrich 37, 44, 74.

ISBN: 0-673-19535-X

Copyright © 1993

Scott, Foresman and Company, Glenview, Illinois.
All Rights Reserved. Printed in the United States of America.

This publication is protected by Copyright and permission should be obtained from the publisher prior to any prohibited reproduction, storage in a retrieval system, or transmission in any form or by any means, electronic, mechanical, photocopying, recording, or otherwise. For information regarding permission, write: Scott, Foresman and Company, 1900 East Lake Avenue, Glenview, Illinois 60025.

6 7 8 9 10 PT 05 04 03 02 01 00

UNIT 1 Buyer Beware?

 PRACTICE 1:
Everywhere You Look

A. Examine the graph. What type of product was advertised the most? Does this surprise you? What other types of advertisements might you see in this type of magazine? Write a few sentences on the lines.

_____

_____

_____

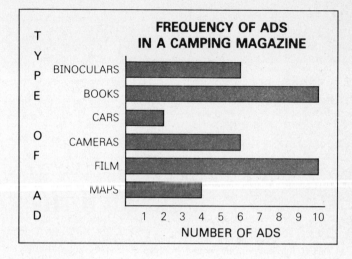

B. Look through a magazine. Graph the frequency of the types of advertisements. What is surprising about your graph? Write a few sentences on a sheet of paper.

T
Y _____
P _____
E _____

O _____
F _____

A
D

NUMBER OF ADS

 PRACTICE 2:
Good Ad? Bad Ad?

A. What is one of your favorite advertisements? Why? Is it humorous? clever? creative? convincing? innovative? artistic? dramatic? true to life? What is one of your least favorite advertisements? Why? Is it sexist? offensive? stupid? irritating? visually unappealing? Write a few sentences on the lines.

_____

_____

B. Work with a group. Do you agree on what makes good advertisements good and bad advertisements bad? Do good ads encourage you to buy the product? Do bad ads encourage you **not** to buy the product? Discuss your answers with two other students.

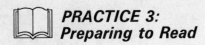 **PRACTICE 3:**
Preparing to Read

Skim and scan the ad to answer the questions. Write the answers on the lines.

1. What is the ad selling? _____

2. What is the main idea of the ad?

_____

3. Does your knowledge about this type of product help you evaluate the ad? How?

_____

GET RICH THE EASY WAY—I DID!

I used to be broke all the time—I never had any money, and I'd live from paycheck to paycheck. It wasn't that I didn't work hard. I had a job with a large industrial company, but I couldn't get ahead. I worked ten and twelve hours a day, but no one noticed. I never got raises. When I suggested ideas, other people got credit. Then I discovered how to get rich the easy way.

Now my problems are over! I live in a mansion in Hollywood, and I own homes in New York and London, which I use to oversee my businesses around the world.

How did I do it? By developing the right mental attitude. You can do it too. My book, *Think Yourself Rich*, tells how the right attitude leads you to success 100 percent of the time. My method does not require huge amounts of money. You only need a few minutes each day to think about the ideas in the book. In a few weeks, you'll be on your way toward developing the same mental attitude I used to succeed.

Try my foolproof method! Join the thousands of people who have tried my method and started building their fortunes.

Send $29.95 plus $3.00 shipping and handling to:

Dr. Tom Brucker
Get Rich Quick Book Offer
1000 Easy Street
Hollywood, California 92121

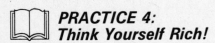 **PRACTICE 4:**
Think Yourself Rich!

Answer the questions. Write your answers on the lines.

1. Do you believe the ad? Why or why not?

_____

2. What kinds of people might believe the ad? Why?

_____

3. What might be the method explained in the book?

_____

PRACTICE 5:
Advertising Double Talk

A. Read the advertising slogans. Match each one with the kind of ad it came from. Write the letter on the line.

_____ **1.** Our business is going downhill, so all weekend trips are half off during January.

_____ **2.** Forest School is offering a class you'll never forget!

_____ **3.** Some parents are letting their children run around in clothes that are half off!

_____ **4.** Stop running away from home!

_____ **5.** We put a lot of energy into our product.

a. a battery ad
b. a Michigan ski resort ad
c. an ad for a sale at a children's clothing store
d. an ad for a beach vacation
e. an ad for a kitchen-cleaning product
f. an ad for memory-improvement lessons

B. What words are being played on? What are their meanings? Complete the chart.

	Word	Meaning 1	Meaning 2
1.			
2.			
3.			
4.			
5.			

PRACTICE 6:
Coin Collection

Write the words used to make each coined word on the line.

1. MediMart Drugstores _____

2. Bargaintel—A Good Place to Stay! _____

3. Try a **Pizzaburger,** the delicious new sandwich from Pizza King!

_____

4. The Family Home Gym is **funbelievable** fitness for the whole family.

_____

 **PRACTICE 7:**
Give Me That Remote!

A. *Many people with remote controls for their TVs no longer watch commercials. They simply change channels. However, constant changing of channels annoys others. How would you persuade someone not to change the channel all the time? How might that person stand his or her ground? Complete the chart.*

Persuade	Stand Ground

B. *Work with a partner. Take turns persuading each other not to change the channel. When your partner tries to persuade you, stand your ground.*

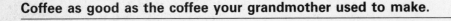 **PRACTICE 8:**
Do You Remember the Way We Were?

Many advertisements try to sell products by appealing to the consumers' nostalgia. The ads emphasize that their products have old-fashioned goodness. Think of four products. Write an ad slogan that appeals to people's sense of the past for each one. Use the habitual past.

Coffee as good as the coffee your grandmother used to make.

_____

_____

_____

_____

PRACTICE 9:
It's Incredibly Innovative!

A. *Write an appropriate intensifier on each line.*

LOU: Did you see that actress promoting her new line of perfume? The

ad was in **(1)** _____ bad taste.

SUE: Oh, did you think so? I thought the commercial was

(2) _____ innovative. And I did think it was

(3) _____ effective.

LOU: Yes, I suppose that type of ad is **(4)** _____ enticing. But

I still think that it's **(5)** _____ disgusting to put ads like

that on TV!

B. *You saw a commercial that you really hated. Write a few lines on a sheet of paper explaining why you disliked the ad. Use intensifiers.*

PRACTICE 10:
Stop the Waste!

A. *The radio program "TalkRadio" is a call-in show. Listen to today's program and circle the answer.*

1. The commercial being discussed
   a. is selling a product.
   b. promotes awareness of a social issue.
   c. is selling a service.

2. Tim Marshall's organization
   a. is enticing people to buy a product.
   b. is promoting the use of coupons.
   c. is encouraging people to consume less.

B. *How would you describe the tone of each participant? Listen again and write an adjective or two on each line.*

George _____

Tim _____

Elaine _____

Bill _____

C. *Work with two or three other students. Discuss the questions.*

1. Would most radio stations accept an ad like this? Why or why not?
2. Who do you agree with—Tim, Elaine, or Bill?
3. Do you think that we consume too much? Why or why not?

PRACTICE 11:
What's It Trying to Sell?

A. *Mark the thought groups with slashes. Then underline the stressed syllable.*

Have you ever watched a commercial or read an advertisement and

wondered what product was being sold? Well, I certainly have. I saw an

ad the other day in which the image was of a group of people sitting

around the breakfast table talking about the good old days. At the very

end was a picture of the product. It was a brand of coffee.

B. *Listen to the paragraph and check your answers. Then work with a partner. Take turns saying the paragraph aloud. Pay attention to the stress and rhythm.*

PRACTICE 12:
Who's the Audience?

A. *Look back at the ad on page 2. What audience is it aimed at? Is it relevant to you? Why or why not? Write your answer on the lines.*

_____

_____

_____

B. *How is the ad written to persuade? Circle the persuasive language. What psychological needs does the ad appeal to? What type of language is used to persuade the reader to send for the book? Write your answer on the lines.*

_____

_____

_____

C. *An ad writer for a book company is trying to choose headlines for ads for three books. Read the pairs of ad headlines. Which headline in each pair is more effective? Circle the correct letter.*

1. a. How to Ruin Your Marriage in the Quickest Possible Way
   b. Your Marriage: How to Live Happily Ever After

2. a. Speaking in Public
   b. Successful Public Speaking in Five Easy Steps

3. a. To a $30,000 Person Who Would Like to Be Making $60,000
   b. Our Training Program Pays Financially

 **PRACTICE 13:**
Panel Discussion

A. In a panel discussion, what language can we use to introduce the participants? to state the goal of the discussion? to open the topic to discussion? Fill in the chart.

Introduce Participants	State Goal	Open the Topic to Discussion

B. Imagine that you are in charge of a panel discussion on whether advertising should be allowed on children's TV programs. Four people—a TV executive, a mother of a young child, a child psychologist, and a school principal—will participate. Write your opening remarks on a sheet of paper. Make sure that you state the goal of the discussion, introduce the speakers, and open the topic to discussion.

PRACTICE 14:
So You Want a Job?

A. You are applying for a research job with an advertising agency. It is extremely important to be able to write well for the job, so you have to pass a writing test. The interviewer has given you a list of possible topics. To organize your work, identify the function and purpose of each topic. Fill in the chart.

Topic	Function	Purpose
1. The importance of public service ads		
2. Which are more effective, TV commercials or magazine ads?		
3. The best commercial of the year		
4. Advertising in the 1980s		
5. Why some commercials work better than others		

B. Use one of the topics to write an essay. Follow the steps of the writing process.

A. Grammar

Write the correct form of the verb on the line. Use the habitual past when appropriate.

In the past, marketers **(1. rely)** _____ on brand loyalty to sell

products. But with hard economic times, everything is changing. Until

recently, consumers **(2. walk)** _____ into a store and

(3. buy) _____ the same product time after time. However,

last year, a study **(4. show)** _____ that these days price

(5. be) _____ more important than brand. In the study,

consumers almost always **(6. choose)** _____ a competing

product instead of their usual brand if the price **(7. be)** _____

lower.

B. Grammar

Write an appropriate intensifier on the line.

Do you want a car that's **(1)** _____ fast? That's

(2) _____ good-looking? And that's **(3)** _____ low

priced? Test-drive a Chevallier today, and soon you'll be driving

(4) _____ the best car on the road!

C. Reading and Writing

The purpose of advertising is to promote products. Some consumers like ads because the ads inform them of products and services, remind them to buy old favorites, and alert them to sales. However, other people feel that ads are an unwelcome invasion of their privacy. How do you feel about ads? Does advertising have a positive or a negative impact on your life? Write a paragraph on a sheet of paper. Follow the steps of the writing process. Then file your paragraph in your writing portfolio.

UNIT 2 A Warming World

PRACTICE 1:
Cleaning Up the Environment

A. Imagine that your town is going to have a cleanup day. People are going to pick up trash, clean parks and rivers, and plant flowers and trees. What areas of town do you think need the most work? Make a list of five places and say what needs to be done in each place.

1. _____

2. _____

3. _____

4. _____

5. _____

B. Compare your list with a partner's. Did you agree on what needs to be done? Who listed the most urgent problems?

PRACTICE 2:
Personal Action

A. What can we do to protect the environment? Read the environmental problems and the list of possible solutions. Write each solution under the problem it could help solve. Then write at least one solution of your own for each problem.

riding a bicycle
planting trees
**reusing plastic bags
  and containers**
riding mass transit

recycling newspapers
buying organic food
**avoiding products that contain
  CFCs**
recycling aluminum cans

Deforestation	Air Pollution	Trash Disposal	Ozone Depletion

B. Work with a partner. Compare your answers. Did you agree? Can some actions be solutions for more than one problem?

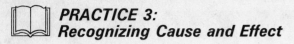

PRACTICE 3:
Recognizing Cause and Effect

*Read "Earth Day: A Time for Reflection and Looking Ahead" and write
four effects that Earth Day has had since 1970.*

1. _____

2. _____

3. _____

4. _____

Earth Day: A Time for Reflection and Looking Ahead

In 1970, as the Vietnam conflict was still waging, a twenty-five-year-old college student named Denis Hayes did something that may have made him the most important environmentalist of our century. He organized lectures, workshops, rallies, and teach-ins, which were held on April 22, 1970. He called it Earth Day. Approximately 20 million people participated in the event across the United States. On April 23, 1990, Earth Day XX was celebrated by over 100 million people in over 100 countries with tree plantings, concerts, TV documentaries, books, festivals, and even a Soviet and Chinese expedition to climb Mount Everest in order to collect garbage left by past expeditions.

The degradation of the environment was not new when the first Earth Days took place. Writers and environmentalists such as Henry David Thoreau, John Muir, and Rachel Carson had already brought it to the public's attention. But the first Earth Days were effective in raising a much wider public awareness than ever before. In the United States, clean air and water laws were passed, and the Environmental Protection Agency (EPA) was founded. In Europe, several "Green"

parties were founded and elected representatives to their governments.

However, the issues have changed since the first Earth Day. In 1970, the pressing environmental issues were trash on highways, smog, and the use of DDT—a chemical used to kill insects that was also killing birds, fish, and other wildlife. In the 1990s, the issues are on a global scale: acid rain, global warming, nuclear contamination, and toxic wastes. The risks are greater too. All of these problems could result in the extinction of the human race. By the fortieth Earth Day, in 2010, we may know the outcome of all these problems. What current problems will have been solved? Will changing people's habits be harder than pulling teeth? We all had better become environmentalists and use our voting and buying power to effect changes. We must direct technological and economic progress toward halting the destruction of the world. Most importantly, we must change our lifestyles. Otherwise, by the fortieth anniversary of Earth Day the human race may be, like the hundreds of animal species we have killed, extinct.

PRACTICE 4:
Distinguishing Fact from Opinion

A. *Are these statements facts or opinions? Write* **F** *for fact or* **O** *for opinion on each line.*

_____ **1.** There is an ozone hole over the South Pole.
_____ **2.** The thinning of the ozone layer is of extreme concern because it poses risks to our health.
_____ **3.** Society must conserve energy in the hope that the buildup of greenhouse gases in the atmosphere can be slowed.
_____ **4.** Over 80 percent of the world's oil reserves will be burned during the lifetime of those currently living.
_____ **5.** CFCs ought to be banned immediately.

B. *Read "Earth Day: A Time for Reflection and Looking Ahead" again and underline three examples of fact and double-underline three of opinion. What words helped you distinguish between them?*

PRACTICE 5:
Root It Out!

Look back at the reading and write at least six words that you think are derived from Latin roots. Then look the words up in the dictionary to find the roots. Were you correct? Write each root on the line. If the root is not Latin, write the language the word is from.

Word	Root
1. _____	_____
2. _____	_____
3. _____	_____
4. _____	_____
5. _____	_____
6. _____	_____

 **PRACTICE 6:**
Dear Pat

A. *In the U.S. people can write to advice columns for solutions to their problems. Read the letter to Pat. Write an answer to Mr. and Mrs. Green on a sheet of paper.*

Dear Pat,

   We try to do environmentally correct things in our home. We recycle newspapers, bottles, cans, plastic, and cardboard. We turn off lights that we aren't using. We use ceiling fans instead of air conditioners. We really are trying to do our best.
   Here's the problem. My in-laws come over a lot, and we've talked to them many times about the things we're trying to do for the environment. However, they leave lights on, and they throw newspapers and bottles into the garbage. I am at my wit's end. They just gave us an air conditioner for Father's Day! We don't want to offend them, but they won't listen to us! What can we do?

                                    Mr. and Mrs. Green

B. *Work with a partner. Take turns playing the roles of Mr. or Mrs. Green and one of the in-laws. Take turns advising and warning each other about not taking care of the environment.*

 PRACTICE 7:
The Garbage Barge

The city has too much garbage and no place to put it because the landfill where the town was burying garbage is full. What can the city do to get rid of its garbage? Write sentences with modals on the lines.

1. _____

2. _____

3. _____

4. _____

5. _____

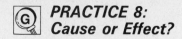

PRACTICE 8:
Cause or Effect?

Read the list of actions that individuals can take to conserve resources. On the lines, write sentences that express each action first as a cause and then as an effect.

I've been riding my bicycle so much lately that I haven't had to fill my car's gas tank in a month. Since I want to use as little gas as possible, I ride my bicycle as much as I can.

1. walking to work
2. lowering the thermostat
3. not using the car air conditioner
4. avoiding products that have unnecessary packaging

1. _____

_____

2. _____

_____

3. _____

_____

4. _____

_____

PRACTICE 9:
A Sunny Future?

Listen to the news program and decide if the following statements are true (T) or false (F).

_____ **1.** The current rate of contracting skin cancer is 1 in 75.

_____ **2.** The occurrence of skin cancer is increasing around the world.

_____ **3.** People can die from skin cancer.

_____ **4.** Sheep in Chile are dying from ultraviolet radiation.

 PRACTICE 10:
Reductions

A. *Read the conversation and underline the words that you think are going to be reduced. Then listen to the conversation. Were your predictions correct?*

A: Where are you going in such a rush?
B: I'm going to the recycling center.
A: Don't you know that it's closed today?
B: Really? I need to get this stuff out of the house.
A: Why don't you give me your stuff? I'm going to go tomorrow.
B: Great. Do you want to go get a bite of lunch with me?

B. *Work with a partner. Read the conversation using the linked and reduced forms.*

 **PRACTICE 11:**
Recognizing Analogies

Read "Earth Day: A Time for Reflection and Looking Ahead" again. What two analogies are made? Write the analogies on the lines.

1. _____

2. _____

 **PRACTICE 12:**
Earth Day 2010

Write two optimistic predictions and two pessimistic predictions about what you think will be happening in the world as Earth Day 2010 nears. Share your predictions with a partner.

Optimistic

1. _____

2. _____

Pessimistic

1. _____

2. _____

 **PRACTICE 13:**
Scrambled Discussions

Here are the opening remarks for two different discussions. Unscramble them and put them in the correct order. Write letters on the lines.

A. It's good to see you all could make it today.
B. I have called this meeting today to inform you of the legal action that has been taken against our company and to discuss possible action.
C. At today's meeting, we need to talk about what each person will do at our information booth on Earth Day.
D. Mr. McDonald, our chief counsel, will begin.
E. The first item on the agenda, the legal action, will be presented by our lawyers.
F. You all know Jim, don't you? He's going to help me conduct the meeting.
G. Seated to my left and right are our company lawyers. Please welcome them.
H. We need to find out two things—your assignment preferences and the times you can work.
I. OK. Let's start. Who wants to help set up?
J. Good evening. Thank you for coming.

Discussion 1   Discussion 2

_____   _____

_____   _____

_____   _____

_____   _____

_____   _____

 PRACTICE 14:
What's the Strategy?

What type of strategy would you use to write an essay in response to each of these questions? Write the answers on the lines.

1. What happened when the town put a recycling program into effect?

_____

2. How have people's habits changed since your city's recycling

program went into effect? _____

3. What is a recycling program? _____

4. Has the new recycling program been a success? _____

5. How are plastics recycled? _____

A. Grammar

Complete the sentences with the appropriate words for expressing cause and effect.

1. Global warming will continue to increase _____ CFCs are

still being used.

2. Trash disposal has become _____ a big problem

_____ many towns don't know what to do with their trash.

3. _____ people are more aware of the need to protect the

environment, participation in recycling programs has increased.

4. _____ people have started recycling, the trash disposal

problem has become less urgent.

5. There are _____ many cars, trucks, and buses on city

streets _____ it is difficult to prevent air pollution from

occurring in our cities.

B. Grammar

A friend of yours wants to change jobs, but this may not be the best time to change jobs because the economy is not very good right now. Tell your friend what you think. Express possibility, certainty, advisability, and necessity.

1. _____

2. _____

3. _____

4. _____

C. Reading and Writing

Many of the problems the earth faces are due to people's desires to move forward, advance, improve, and live more comfortable lives. Perhaps our society moved too quickly. Or perhaps problems such as global warming couldn't have been predicted. What is more important, economic growth and progress or protecting the environment? Would you be willing to accept a lower standard of living to protect the environment? Write a short essay. Follow all of the steps of the writing process. When you are finished, file your essay in your writing portfolio.

UNIT **3** In Left Field

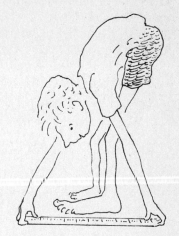

PRACTICE 1:
My Left Foot

Are you right-handed or left-handed? Do you do some things with one hand and other things with the other? Or can you use both hands equally well?

Did you know that people who are right-handed are usually right-footed and right-eyed too? Take these simple tests to find out which side of your body is dominant.

Test 1: *Hands*
Draw two circles, one with your left hand and one with your right. In which direction did you draw the circles—clockwise or counterclockwise? Or did you draw one of each?

_____

Test 2: *Eyes*
Look at a point across the room. Extend your arm and hold up one finger so it covers the point. Close one eye first and then the other. With which eye open did your finger still cover the point?

_____

Test 3: *Feet*
Stand in the middle of the room. Slowly lean forward until you start to lose your balance. Stop yourself from falling by stepping forward with one foot. Which foot did you instinctively use?

_____

Test 4: *Feet*
Measure and write down the length and width of each of your feet. Are they the same size, or is one larger?
Left foot: width _____   length _____
Right foot: width _____   length _____

Test 5: *Legs*
Sit down and cross your legs. Which leg is on top?

_____

Answers

Test 5: Your dominant leg is probably on top.
Test 4: Your dominant foot is probably the larger.
Test 3: You probably stepped forward with your dominant foot.
Test 2: Your answer probably names your dominant eye.
Test 1: If you drew either or both of your circles in a clockwise direction, you have an inclination toward left-handedness.

PRACTICE 2:
On the Other Hand

A. *Superstitions and expressions about left and right exist in almost every culture and language. For example, in Scotland it is considered good luck to put your pants on right leg first and bad luck to put them on left leg first. If you can't dance well, English speakers say you have "two left feet." The same speakers, however, may believe that seeing a new moon over your left shoulder is lucky. Think of superstitions and expressions that you know about left and right, either in English or in your native language. Classify them as positive or negative.*

Positive	**Negative**
_____	_____
_____	_____
_____	_____
_____	_____

B. *Do you think any of these superstitions or expressions have a basis in reality? What do you think these superstitions and expressions reflect about the world? Share your ideas with a partner.*

C. *Work in a group. Pretend you live in a world in which most people are left-handed. Make up two superstitions or expressions. Share your ideas with the class. Which idea is the most creative? the funniest? the most interesting?*

_____

_____

 **PRACTICE 3:**
Preparing to Read

A. *The article on page 19 is about how the brain affects right- and left-handedness. Use what you already know about the brain to predict something the article might say.*

_____

_____

In Defense of Left-Handers

In recent years, left-handers have been seen wearing T-shirts with this slogan:

> If the left side of the brain controls the right hand, and the right side of the brain controls the left hand, then only left-handers are in their right mind.

This may be only partially a joke. Left-handers are often more perceptive, creative, adaptable, independent, and determined than their right-handed colleagues. Brain research has shown that the left hemisphere of the brain (which controls the right side of the body) is the more verbal and analytical side. The right hemisphere (which controls the left side) holds the keys to perception and creativity. For example, the right hemisphere allows humans to brainstorm, that is, to look at all facets of a problem and not be stuck with only a few alternatives.

Therefore it does not come as a surprise that some research has shown that left-handers tend to have more acute visual perception and better spatial competence than right-handers. For example, professional architects and architecture students were studied at the University of Cincinnati. The results indicated that many lefties had a better sense of proportion and distance than would be "normally expected."

Another study, at Boston University, showed that lefties are more determined and more inclined to try to figure things out than righties, who more often believe what others tell them. (This could be a reason lefties have the reputation of being stubborn and contrary.)

As research continues, it may show that for many kinds of thinking, the T-shirt slogan is correct—left is right!

B. *Was your prediction about the article correct? Was there any information in the article that surprised you? Share your ideas with a partner.*

C. *Work with a partner. Based on the information in the article, what jobs do you think left-handers would be better at than right-handers? Why?*

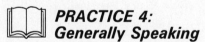 **PRACTICE 4:**
Generally Speaking

A. *Circle the examples of generalization in "In Defense of Left-Handers." Then choose one generalization and, based on your knowledge and any scientific evidence given, tell why you agree or disagree with the generalization.*

_____

_____

B. *Underline statements in the article that are qualified. Do you think any of these statements could be proven true beyond a reasonable doubt? Share your ideas with a partner.*

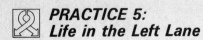
*Write the correct word with **-ever** on each line.*

My sister Jill is the only lefty in our family. Some things, like learning

how to tie her shoes, were hard for her. **(1)** _____ a right-

handed person tried to teach her, she couldn't figure it out. Finally our

left-handed neighbor showed her how. Eating can be difficult for her

too. She can't sit **(2)** _____ she wants at the table. She has to

sit at the end so her elbow doesn't hit **(3)** _____ is sitting next

to her. Even at school she had a hard time. Her teachers complained

because **(4)** _____ Jill held her pencil, her writing was not very

legible. One teacher even tried to make her change hands

(5) _____ he saw her writing with her left hand.

PRACTICE 6:
So What's Your Complaint?

A. *Choose one of the following situations. On the lines, write some polite complaints you would make.*

1. A friend always jokes about your clumsiness, and you're getting tired of it.
2. Your hairdresser/barber didn't cut your hair the way you wanted it cut.
3. Your roommate leaves his/her things all over the apartment and then asks you where they are.
4. A classmate loves to whisper to you while the teacher is talking.
5. your own idea

_____

_____

_____

_____

B. *Work with a partner. Complain about the situation you chose and try to resolve the problem.*

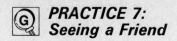

PRACTICE 7:
Seeing a Friend

*Read each sentence. If possible, reduce the clause and rewrite the sentence with a participial phrase. If this is not possible, write **NP**.*

1. Since I hadn't seen Ravi for a while, I invited him to dinner.

_____

2. As I was entering the restaurant, I noticed it had been redecorated.

_____

3. When Ravi arrived, the waiter brought us our menus.

_____

4. While I was reading the menu, I became very embarrassed.

_____

5. When the designer finished decorating the restaurant, the owners raised all the prices.

_____

6. After I checked my wallet, I told Ravi we had to leave.

_____

PRACTICE 8:
Showing Contrast

A. *Choose one of the following pairs of items and think of at least five differences between them. Write sentences using clauses to show contrast.*

right-handers and left-handers
people who exercise and couch potatoes
the opera and rock and roll
TV and the movies

_____

_____

_____

_____

_____

B. *Ask a partner to read your sentences. Does your partner agree with what you wrote? Why or why not?*

PRACTICE 9:
Left or Right?

A. *Listen to the lecture. What is the main idea?*

_____

B. *Listen again. Complete the sentences.*

1. In the French National Assembly, _____ sat on the right,

and _____ sat on the left.

2. Aristotle wrote that the Greeks considered that what is on the

_____ is good and what is on the _____ is bad.

3. The word _____ is derived from a Greek word which means

_____ or "those qualified to _____ ."

4. Early Roman priests faced _____ to worship because that is

to the _____ of where the sun rises.

5. The Zuñi people believed that the _____ side was the wiser side.

PRACTICE 10:
Do You Agree?

Listen to the question. Circle the letter of the correct intonation. Then write a logical response.

1. a. Rising   **b.** Falling _____

2. a. Rising   **b.** Falling _____

3. a. Rising   **b.** Falling _____

4. a. Rising   **b.** Falling _____

5. a. Rising   **b.** Falling _____

PRACTICE 11:
Supporting Examples

A. *Reread "In Defense of Left-Handers" on page 19. What is the main idea? Underline the best answer.*

1. Right-handers have a natural bias against left-handers.

2. Left-handers have some advantages over right-handers.

3. Bias against left-handers should stop.

B. *Classify these ideas from the article as fact or opinion. Write F (fact) or O (opinion) on each line. Underline those ideas that support the main idea of the article.*

_____ **1.** Left-handers tend to have more acute visual perception than right-handers.

_____ **2.** Lefties had a better sense of proportion than would be "normally expected."

_____ **3.** Righties more often believe what others tell them.

_____ **4.** Lefties have the reputation of being stubborn.

PRACTICE 12:
Keep It Going

Work with a group. You are to design a tool that will make life easier for left-handers. First, decide on a tool; then figure out how you will make it work better for left-handers. For example, you might decide to design a pencil sharpener that turns in the opposite direction of normal pencil sharpeners. Use appropriate expressions to keep the discussion moving. Take notes on the different ideas presented, the idea finally chosen, and the reasons for the choice.

PRACTICE 13:
In Summary

Group leaders or secretaries often write summaries of discussions. Use the notes you took for Practice 12 and write a summary of the discussion. Write a rough draft here and ask a partner to check it for content, clarity, and organization. Then write your final version on a sheet of paper.

_____

_____

_____

_____

_____

_____

_____

_____

_____

_____

A. Grammar

Read each sentence. If possible, reduce the clause and rewrite the sentence with a participial phrase. If this is not possible, write NP.

1. After I read about left-handers, I became more aware of their problems.

_____

2. Since I'm right-handed, I hadn't thought about this before.

_____

3. While I was watching my left-handed sister cook, I realized that new utensils need to be designed.

_____

4. Since the spout was on the wrong side of the ladle, she couldn't pour things easily.

_____

B. Grammar

Combine the ideas in each item using structures of contrast.

1. Left-handers are considered clumsy.
Many sports stars are left-handed.

_____

_____

2. Life would be easier for left-handers if tools were designed specifically for their use.
Not many companies make left-handed tools.

_____

_____

C. Reading and Writing

Left-handers are not the only minority that has been stereotyped because of a physical difference. Many people also make generalities about people with red hair, people who are unusually tall or short, or people who are fatter or thinner than the ideal norm. Choose one of these minorities. What generalizations do people make about this minority? Do you agree or disagree with the generalizations? Why? Write a paragraph on a sheet of paper. Follow the steps of the writing process. File your paragraph in your writing portfolio.

UNIT 4 Word to the World

PRACTICE 1:
Riddles

A. *Read the riddles. Think about the play on words in each one. Can you make the same play on words in your native language?*

1. Which is the highest building in any city?
   The library—it has the most stories.
2. How can you spell *mousetrap* in only three letters?
   C-A-T.
3. Why did the boy's mother buy him three new shoes?
   Because in the last year, he'd grown a foot.

B. *Choose one of the riddles to tell in your native language. Can you translate it exactly, or will you have to change something in order for the riddle to make sense? Explain.*

_____

_____

_____

C. *Think of a joke or riddle you know in a language other than English. Translate the joke into English and tell it to a partner or to the class.*

PRACTICE 2:
Double Translation

A. *Write a sentence or two about a time you experienced joy—or frustration—when trying to communicate in English.*

_____

_____

B. *Work with two other students with whom you share a language besides English. Take turns being Student A, Student B, and Student C. Student A whispers his or her statement from **A** to Student B. Student B translates the statement into another language and whispers it to Student C. Student C translates the statement back into English and says it aloud. Write Student C's version of your statement.*

_____

_____

C. *How close was Student C's version to your original statement? What does this tell you about translation? Share your ideas with your group.*

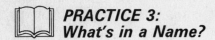

PRACTICE 3:
What's in a Name?

A. *In Shakespeare's play* Romeo and Juliet, *the two main characters are in love, but they come from families who are enemies—Romeo is a Montague, and Juliet is a Capulet. Read Juliet's speech to Romeo.*

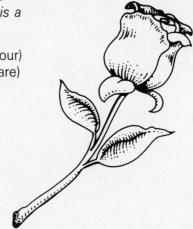

'Tis but thy name that is my enemy;   (*'tis* = it is; *thy* = your)
Thou art thyself, though not a Montague.   (*thou* = you; *art* = are)
What's Montague? It is nor hand, nor foot,
Nor arm, nor face, nor any other part
Belonging to a man. O, be some other name!
What's in a name? That which we call a rose
By any other word would smell as sweet;
So Romeo would, were he not Romeo call'd,   (*call'd* = called)
Retain that dear perfection which he owes   (*owes* = owns)
Without that title. Romeo, doff thy name,   (*doff* = take off)
And for thy name, which is no part of thee,   (*thee* = you)
Take all myself.

B. *Compare Shakespeare's ideas about names with Pablo Neruda's in "Too Many Names" on page 39 of the Student Book. Do you think the writers basically agree or disagree? Discuss your ideas with a partner.*

C. *"A rose by any other name would smell as sweet" has become a famous saying in English. Translators frequently avoid giving a literal translation of a saying. Instead, they give an equivalent saying in the second language. Do you know a saying in a language other than English that means approximately the same as this one? Write it here along with its literal translation.*

_____

_____

PRACTICE 4:
Fine Lines

Classify each word in a group as positive (+), negative (-), or neutral (0). Compare your ideas with a partner's.

1. eat _____   dine _____   gobble _____

2. well-to-do _____   rich _____   loaded _____

3. canine _____   dog _____   mutt _____

4. pig-headed _____   firm _____   obstinate _____

5. inquisitive _____   nosy _____   curious _____

PRACTICE 5:
Is a Chair a Chair?

A. *The word* **chair** *denotes "a seat that has a back, usually for one person," but* **chair** *connotes different things to different people. Who might make each of these statements? Write the answers on the lines.*

1. "You'll get the chair for this, you dirty rat," snarled the

_____ .

2. "I play first chair in the flute section," said the _____ .

3. "Miss Habib will be the chair of the new publicity committee

for our club," announced the _____ .

4. "I hope to be made chair of the philosophy department at Hope

College," said the _____ .

B. *You want to translate each statement in* **A** *into your native language. What word will you use for* **chair** *in each one?*

PRACTICE 6:
Be Tactful

A. *You and a friend are taking driver's education. Your friend isn't doing very well and has come to you for help. Offer some constructive criticism and tell how it could be paraphrased in a response. Fill in the chart.*

B. *Work with a partner. Take turns criticizing each other's driving. Respond with a paraphrase when possible.*

	Criticism	Paraphrase
neglects to use turn signals		
drives too fast		
drives in middle of road		
plays radio too loud		
forgets to check rearview mirror		

PRACTICE 7:
Limericks

A. *A limerick is a type of nonsense poem. These three limericks are by Edward Lear, perhaps the most famous writer of limericks. Circle the relative clause in each. Underline the noun phrase the relative pronoun refers to.*

There was an Old Man of Moldavia,
who had the most curious behavior;
For while he was able,
he slept on a table,
That funny Old Man of Moldavia.

There was an Old Person of Dutton,
whose head was as small as a button;
So to make it look big,
he purchased a wig,
And rapidly rushed about Dutton.

There was a Young Lady of Troy,
whom several large Flies did annoy;
Some she killed with a thump,
some she drowned at the pump,
And some she took with her to Troy.

B. *Use the limericks on page 27 to analyze the elements of a limerick.*

1. Number of lines: _____

2. Lines that rhyme: _____ , _____ , and _____ ; _____ and _____

3. Number of stresses in lines 1, 2, and 5: _____

4. Number of stresses in lines 3 and 4: _____

C. *Write a limerick of your own. Use the name of a place at the end of line 1 and a relative pronoun in line 2.*

PRACTICE 8: . . . , Which Was Disappointing

Complete each sentence with a clause that the which *clause can modify. Don't forget to use a comma.*

1. _____ which was a surprise.

2. _____ which was quite understandable.

3. _____ which I didn't appreciate at all.

4. _____ which was rather foolish of them.

5. _____ which she'll really enjoy.

PRACTICE 9: The Art of Translation

A. *Rewrite each sentence with a reduced clause.*

1. One translator who is considered a great novelist in his own right is Vladimir Nabokov.

_____

2. The author of many books that were written in English, Joseph Conrad was a native speaker

of Polish. _____

3. The woman who was hired yesterday to be a simultaneous interpreter at the UN was in my class

in high school. _____

4. The limericks that were written by the students were very creative.

_____

5. The translation that was done for the museum brochure was full of mistakes.

_____

B. *Expand each sentence with a relative clause.*

1. The whole section misinterpreted by the translator must be redone by tomorrow.

_____

2. The actors awarded Oscars appeared in some very popular movies.

_____

3. Did you enjoy the short story read on public radio last night?

_____

4. The English translation, considered to be well written, completely missed the point of the poem.

_____

5. Did you understand the consequences implied by the ending?

_____

 PRACTICE 10:
Tales Across Cultures

A. *Similar fairy tales and fable are told in different cultures. Do you think the same stories are translated into different languages, or do you think people in different cultures think up similar plots? Share your ideas with the class.*

raven   lobster   fox

B. *Listen to the conversation. Fill in the chart.*

	Story 1	*Story 2*
1. Where is the story from?		
2. Who are the two main characters?		
3. What is the problem?		
4. How is the problem solved?		

C. *Listen to the conversation again. What is the moral of the stories?*

_____

D. *Do you know a similar story from your culture? Tell it to a partner or to the class.*

PRACTICE 11:
Different by a Sound

*Work with a partner. One person takes part **A,** and the other person takes part **B** in the box at the bottom of the page. Read the sentences to each other. As one person reads, the other circles the word in the second column that he or she hears.*

Part A

1. Do you know the price for this game?	**1.** dish	ditch
2. Could I borrow a red pencil?	**2.** eat	heat
3. We have to get out the vote.	**3.** thin	tin
4. I need you to mash the potatoes.	**4.** cheer	jeer
5. Can you tell me what she thought?	**5.** locked	rocked

PRACTICE 12:
A Poet's Style

A. *Humorous poets often use unusual spellings or pronunciations to help make their work funny. Look at the first limerick on page 27. What word does Edward Lear rhyme with **Moldavia?***

B. *Ogden Nash is famous for spelling words in unusual ways to make them rhyme. What word has an odd spelling in this poem?*

The Panther
by Ogden Nash

The panther is like a leopard,
Except it hasn't been peppered.
Should you behold a panther crouch,
Prepare to say Ouch.
Better yet, if called by a panther,
Don't anther.

C. *Compare the tone and style of Nash's poem about the panther with that of Rilke's poem on page 48 of your Student Book. Would Nash's poem be easy to translate into your native language? Why or why not? Share your ideas with a partner.*

Part B

1. There's water in the dish.	**1.** price	prize
2. Did Lars heat the soup?	**2.** lead	red
3. Hand me that thin platter.	**3.** boat	vote
4. Did you hear the audience jeer?	**4.** mash	match
5. She rocked the baby on the porch.	**5.** taught	thought

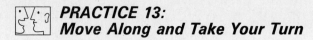

PRACTICE 13:
Move Along and Take Your Turn

A. *Read the following expressions and classify them according to function.*

Moving along to the next speaker, . . .
Let's go on to the next problem.
Does anyone want to make a comment?
Any more suggestions before we continue?
Let's hear what Amalia thinks about it.
We still have a lot to talk about, so let's move on.
May I say something?
To bring up the last issue, . . .

Keeping a Discussion Going	Taking Turns

B. *How are keeping a discussion going and taking turns similar? different? What expressions could be used for either function? Write a few expressions.*

_____

_____

PRACTICE 14:
After the First Draft

A. *A friend has written the first draft of an essay on language and has asked for your help. Edit this paragraph and write a second draft on a sheet of paper.*

Although we are more exposed to spoken language, we are more aware of written language. In fact, more efforts to improve our language use and knowledge are through writing materials. In some ways the written words can be more powerful than the spoken message. It lasts an eternity, whereas the fleeting life of a sound wave. Philosophers of days long ago yet influence our thinking though the written page. The written language conveys more complete and organized thoughts then spoken language because ideas have been thought out, reworked and polished before they set to paper. The written word also conveys more complex ideas. These ideas, if communicate orally, would be confusing or unfollowable. The written word allows the language user to go back a seconder and third time for to understand an idea.

B. *Work with a partner. Exchange your edited paragraphs and offer constructive criticism. Then write a final version of the paragraph.*

A. Grammar

Combine each pair of sentences. Use a relative pronoun.

1. The poetry class is conducted in Russian. The class is difficult for me.

_____

2. The translator can use poetic license. His knowledge of the language and culture is deep.

_____

3. The translation was done by Jorge Luis Borges. It's one of the best I've read.

_____

4. The play was performed by the students. It was written by Shakespeare.

_____

5. Maria is studying to be a playwright. Her paper about Greek tragedies won the recent essay contest.

_____

B. Grammar

Look at the sentences you wrote for **A.** *Rewrite those in which the relative clauses can be reduced to phrases.*

_____

_____

_____

_____

C. Reading and Writing

Many of the great Russian writers—such as Pasternak, Dostoevski, Pushkin, Nabokov, and Akmatova—were also highly regarded translators. In fact, translation is considered a very special art in Russia, and the names of translators are often as well known as the original writers. Do you think translators of poetry and other literature need to be great writers in their own right? Why or why not? Do you think great books attract great translators? Write a short essay explaining your ideas. Follow the steps of the writing process. Then file your paragraph in your writing portfolio.

PRACTICE 1:
Reasons to Marry

A. Write a list of at least five reasons that people marry.

_____   _____

_____   _____

_____   _____

_____   _____

_____   _____

B. Which five reasons in **A** are meaningful to you? Rank them from most important **(1)** to least important **(5).**

C. Compare your ideas with a partner's. How are your opinions different? similar? Explain why you ranked your ideas as you did.

PRACTICE 2:
May I Quote You on That?

A. Read each quote and decide if it is positive **(P)** or negative **(N)** about marriage. Write the letter on the line.

_____ **1.** "A happy marriage is a long conversation which always seems too short." Andre Maurois

_____ **2.** "Marriage is a great institution, but I'm not ready for an institution yet." Mae West

_____ **3.** "Familiarity breeds contentment." George Ade

_____ **4.** "Though familiarity may not breed contempt, it takes the edge off admiration." William Hazlitt

_____ **5.** "All any woman asks of her husband is that he love her and obey her commandments." John W. Roper

B. Work with a partner. Choose one of the quotes and explain why you agree or disagree with it. Try to persuade your partner to your point of view.

Andre Maurois   Mae West   William Hazlitt

PRACTICE 3:
Organizational Patterns

A. *Read the book review. On page 35, draw a diagram of its organizational pattern.*

Intercultural Marriage
by Judy Mendel

Making a marriage work is difficult at the best of times, even for people of the same cultural background. What happens then when two people from different cultures decide to marry? In *Intercultural Marriage: Promises and Pitfalls* (Intercultural Press, 1988), Dugan Romano does not attempt to solve the problems of what she terms "intercultural marriage," but rather, she points out potential areas of conflict so couples can understand the "extra effort" that may be needed to avoid conflict. This book can be helpful both to intercultural couples who are contemplating marriage and to those who are already married.

Romano suggests that members of such couples reflect on factors and situations in their own lives at the time they were attracted to each other. For example, how did the partners feel about themselves—confident? insecure? shy? lonely? nationalistic? What was happening in their lives? Were they under stress? What are the feelings in their cultures about foreigners and even about other ethnic groups? What are their cultures' ideas about family relationships and about the expectations and goals of marriage?

Romano then describes seven personality types of people who are likely to enter an intercultural marriage. (See Chart A.) She emphasizes that any one person is probably made up of more than one of these types. Romano suggests that reflecting on their motives for marriage and on their personality types can help couples recognize possible danger areas. (See Chart B.) Then, after learning as much as they can about each other's culture, couples are equipped to have some "serious one-on-one discussions."

Romano is very thorough in her assessments, using real-life examples from intercultural couples she interviewed. She also includes a list of factors that the couples themselves believe contribute to successful marriages. (See Chart C.) Many of her analyses, theories, and ideas seem to be firmly based on family therapy training. What struck me after reading this book was that it may be useful not only for couples from different cultures, but for all couples. After all, the big-city boy and the small-town girl are culturally different as well.

Chart A

Types of People Who Enter Intercultural Marriages	
rebels	mavericks
compensators	adventurers
outcasts	escapists
unstable people	

Chart B

Potential Pitfalls for Intercultural Couples	
values	food and drink
religion	ethnocentrism
time	place of residence
friends	raising children
finances	male/female roles
in-laws	language/communication
politics	illness and suffering
social class	dealing with stress

Chart C

Factors for Success in Intercultural Marriage
good motives for marriage
common goals
sensitivity to the other's needs
flexibility
a liking for the other's culture
solid, positive self-image
spirit of adventure
sense of humor
commitment to the relationship
ability to communicate

Diagram of Organizational Pattern:

B. *Answer the questions based on the charts on page 34.*

1. Why do you think each type of person named might be likely to enter an intercultural marriage? Write your answer on a sheet of paper.
2. Circle the factors for success in an intercultural marriage that you think are factors for success in all marriages.
3. Circle the potential pitfalls for intercultural couples that you think might be pitfalls for any couple.

C. *Work with a partner. Compare your answers to* **B.** *Do you more often agree or disagree?*

PRACTICE 4:
Do-It-Yourself Weddings

A. *Add an appropriate suffix to each word in dark type and write the new word on the line. Make nouns plural when necessary.*

Some engaged couples come to the **(1. realize)** _____

that the **(2. convention)** _____ wedding ceremony might

not be for them. Therefore, many couples are now

(3. enthusiastic) _____ writing their own vows in order

to **(4. deep)** _____ their significance, using a

(5. combine) _____ of **(6. tradition)** _____

and modern elements. These couples may choose new

(7. select) _____ of music and new seating

(8. arrange) _____ as well.

B. *Write the word-class change that occurred for each example.*

1. _____   **5.** _____

2. _____   **6.** _____

3. _____   **7.** _____

4. _____   **8.** _____

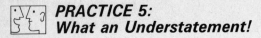

PRACTICE 5:
What an Understatement!

A. *Underline the expressions of understatement.*

BRIDE: Mom, I really don't think we need such a fancy place for the wedding.

MOTHER: Nonsense. The Grand Imperial Ballroom is nothing more than an ordinary dining room.

BRIDE: And the flowers are way too expensive!

MOTHER: Why, they're just a small expression of beauty, don't you think? And the eight-course wedding banquet is only a modest symbol that you care about your guests.

BRIDE: Mom, you're the queen of understatement!

B. *What tone does the mother use? Is she serious or sarcastic? What makes you think so? Work with a partner. Take turns reading the roles of the bride and the mother. Try using different tones of voice.*

PRACTICE 6:
Wedding Customs

Use the words in parentheses to complete each sentence about wedding customs. Use an appropriate passive construction.

1. (bride's and groom's wrists/bind together with grass)

In some parts of Africa _____

2. (gifts/wrap in red)

In China, _____ , the color of love and joy.

3. (sugared almonds/toss at the bride and groom)

In Italy _____

4. (bride/adorn with makeup and jewels)

In Morocco, _____

5. (white silk cord/drape around couple's shoulders)

In the Philippines, _____

6. (thyme/sew into groom's clothes)

In Sweden, _____ to scare away trolls.

 ### PRACTICE 7:
The State of Things

The wedding banquet was delicious, but now everything is in a mess.
Write at least five sentences to describe the picture. Use the stative passive.

_____

_____

_____

PRACTICE 8:
Here's to You!

A. *A toast is the act of drinking to someone's good health or fortune.*
Toasts can be as short and casual as "Here's to you" in English or
"Salud" in Spanish, or they can be quite long and formal. What are
some occasions at which toasts are made? What are some examples of
toasts from your culture? Share your ideas with the class.

B. *Listen to the toast and answer the questions.*

1. Who is being toasted? _____

2. What is the relationship of the person giving the toast to those who are being toasted? _____

3. To whom did the person giving the toast go for advice? _____

4. What advice did he get? _____

C. *Listen to the toast again and give examples of when the toastmaster*
used each of these tones.

1. humorous _____

_____

2. serious _____

_____

3. romantic _____

_____

PRACTICE 9:
A Contract for the Future

A. *Read the dialogue. Underline the stressed words or syllables and mark the intonation patterns with arrows.*

MARGARET: Dave, I hate to bring this up, but what do you think about making a prenuptial contract?

DAVE: Margaret, do you really think that's necessary? You believe that marriage is a lifetime commitment, don't you?

MARGARET: Certainly. But in these times, aren't you afraid of what might happen? We might have problems with money, careers, or in-laws. We could even disagree about how to raise the children, couldn't we?

DAVE: Of course not! What are you afraid of? I love you and will forever. Nothing will get in the way of that!

MARGARET: That's why I love you, Dave. You're really an idealist, aren't you?

B. *Listen to the dialogue and check your answers.*

PRACTICE 10:
Relating Information

A. *Look at the book review on page 34. Do the charts summarize the information in the review or provide additional information? Why do you think the author included the charts? Share your ideas with a partner.*

B. *On the line before each statement write whether it's true (T) or false (F) according to Romano. On the line after each statement, write where you found the answer—in the review (R), the charts (C), or both (B).*

_____ **1.** People who reflect on their motives for marriage often recognize politics as a possible pitfall. _____

_____ **2.** Adventurers and rebels often enter intercultural marriages. _____

_____ **3.** Any one person is probably a combination of personality types. _____

_____ **4.** Intercultural couples identify being flexible and having common goals as factors that contribute to a successful marriage. _____

PRACTICE 11:
Digressing

A. *Work with a partner. Brainstorm a context in which each digression might be made and write it after the statement.*

1. Incidentally, how is your brother doing? _____

_____

2. Before you continue, I'd like to remind you that you owe me money.

_____

3. By the way, I forgot to tell you about the letter I got today. _____

_____

B. *With your partner, choose one of the contexts and make up a conversation that uses the digression.*

PRACTICE 12:
Types of Notes

Classify the note cards according to type: summary **(S),** *paraphrase* **(PA),** *personal* **(PE),** *or quotation* **(Q).**

1. _____
> Klausner, Abraham J. (1986). *Weddings: A Complete Guide to All Religious and Interfaith Marriage Services.* Columbus, OH: Alpha Publishing Company, p. 5
>
> "A wedding is a 'reaching out' experience. Guests are invited to witness the marriage. They constitute the select community in which the marriage is pronounced. The formal or public service and its celebration is also for them. It is not only proper, but imperative, that the feelings and sensitivities of the guests be considered in planning the wedding."

2. _____
> —ask Joanna's sister (the florist) what she tells brides at a wedding interview

3. _____
> *Bride's New Way to Wed* (1990). eds. of *Bride's* magazine with Antonia Van der Meer, New York: Perigee Books, pp. 30–31
>
> lists the possible configurations of the processional

4. _____
> Romano, Dugan (1988). *Intercultural Marriages: Promises and Pitfalls,* Yarmouth, Maine: Intercultural Press, pp. 34–39
>
> Eating customs (the what, the where, the when, and the how) can vary greatly between cultures. Depending on the openness of people, mealtimes can become times for serious conflict.

UNIT 5 CHECK YOUR KNOWLEDGE

A. Grammar

Write an appropriate passive construction on each line.

1. In the United States, wedding licenses _____ by the

government.

2. The wedding ceremony _____ by a judge or a member

of the clergy.

3. Wedding rings _____ by the bride and groom.

4. The wedding dinner _____ by the bride's parents.

5. Gifts _____ to the bride and groom by their friends

and families.

B. Grammar

Write an appropriate stative passive on each line.

Everything is ready for the wedding dinner. The cake

(1) _____ , the flowers **(2)** _____ , and the

tables **(3)** _____ . The waiters' ties

(4) _____ and their shoes **(5)** _____ . As

soon as the meals **(6)** _____, the party will begin.

C. Reading and Writing

If you were planning your own wedding, what kind of wedding would you like to have? Make some personal notes in the space below. Then write an essay about your ideal wedding. Follow the steps of the writing process. When you are finished, file your essay in your writing portfolio.

UNIT 6 That's Entertainment!

 PRACTICE 1:
What's It All About?

Moviemaking is not a simple process. How many different aspects of moviemaking can you think of? Make an idea map.

| moviemaking |

PRACTICE 2:
Some Like It Hot

A. *When people leave a movie theater, some of them comment on how the cinematography caught their attention. Others focus on the dialogue or the direction. What captures your interest in a movie? What makes a movie entertaining? List the factors that make you come out of the theater saying, "That was a good movie."*

_____

_____

_____

B. *Read what these moviemakers said about elements of moviemaking. Which do you agree with? Why? Write a brief opinion for each statement.*

1. Anyone can direct a good picture if he's got a good script.
                                        —*Garson Kanin, screenwriter*

_____

2. The best films are best because of nobody but the director.
                                        —*Roman Polanski, director*

_____

3. I care nothing about the story, only how it is photographed and presented.   —*Josef von Sternberg, director and screenwriter*

_____

4. On a film set, the only person less important than a director is a talent agent.   —*John Cassavetes, actor and director*

_____

5. A good film is when the price of the dinner, the theater admission, and the baby-sitter were worth it.
                                        —*Alfred Hitchcock, director and producer*

_____

C. *Think of the last movie you saw that you really liked. What did you like about it? List some ideas; then share them with a partner.*

_____

_____

_____

_____

PRACTICE 3:
Animation

A. *What do* Fantasia, Beauty and the Beast, *and* Who Framed Roger Rabbit? *have in common? Where else have you seen animation? List a few movies, TV shows, or commercials.*

_____

_____

_____

B. *As you read the article, determine the tone and the level of formality. Underline the words and phrases that help you decide.*

Creating Life

When most people hear the word *animation,* they probably think of cartoons, but there are many more genres that take advantage of the possibilities of this moviemaking technique—TV commercials, videos, promotional pieces for agencies such as NASA, and special-effects sequences in regular, live-action movies. Animation has come a long way from the black-and-white stick figures of Winsor McKay's *Gertie the Dinosaur* in 1909 to the amazing color and movement of Walt Disney's *Fantasia* in 1940 to the computer techniques of the first Oscar-nominated animated feature film *Beauty and the Beast* in 1991.

Animation has traditionally been a slow process, accomplished frame by frame by animators using a variety of media—pen or pencil, clay, puppets, or anything else that can be manipulated. The majority of cartoons and animated movies are made through the tedious process of creating thousands of separate drawings and using the cel method of production. In this method, the artist first makes layout sketches of the major elements for each frame of the sequence. When the sketches are complete, each must be traced, or "inked," on a rectangular sheet of cellulose acetate, or "cel." Each frame may consist of several different cels, one on top of the other, each with a different part of the final picture. (For example, the background sky may be on one cel, a clump of trees on another, and a prowling cat on a third.) After all the cels are inked, they must be painted. And finally, everything is photographed. The rapid succession of the frames through a projector creates the illusion of movement.

Today, the field of animation has changed, just as everything else that has been touched by technology has changed. Computers will probably never completely replace the traditional hand-drawn illustrations, but they can do much of the time-consuming work faster and more accurately. Animators are using computers to ink and paint more precisely. The computer's ability to scan and reproduce images enables animators to create lush backgrounds, full of color and texture. And animators can use computers to create extremely realistic three-dimensional images. In fact, animators can use digital technology to manipulate drawings, photos, and almost anything else in ways that would be impractical for artists to do on light tables.

You have probably already seen advanced computer animation in TV commercials and in movies like *Terminator 2: Judgment Day,* in which a character emerges from a floor in one scene and walks through a wall of fire in another. However, don't look for more than a few seconds of computer animation in any one feature film. The eye-catching techniques can cost $500,000 per minute, and the result can take weeks longer to produce than a live-action shot.

Arnold Schwarzenegger in
Terminator 2: Judgment Day

 **PRACTICE 4:**
Organizing Information

Scan the article to complete the chart.

Examples of Animated Films	
Examples of Animation Techniques	
Examples of Animation Terminology	
Examples of Computer Technology in Animation	

PRACTICE 5:
Why Did They Call It That?

A. *Which language do you think each of these words came from?*
Match the word with the language. If you don't know for sure, try to
guess the answers. Don't check a dictionary yet.

_____ **1.** alligator

_____ **2.** catsup

_____ **3.** cheetah

_____ **4.** chimpanzee

_____ **5.** coffee

_____ **6.** kimono

_____ **7.** llama

_____ **8.** moccasin

_____ **9.** parka

_____ **10.** spaghetti

_____ **11.** squash

_____ **12.** tea

a. Italian
b. Malay
c. Chinese
d. Arabic
e. Narragansett
f. Hindustani
g. Spanish
h. Japanese
i. Bantu
j. Quechua
k. Russian
l. Algonquian

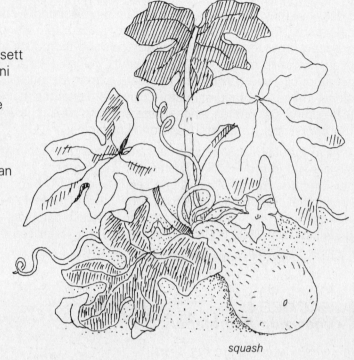

squash

B. *Work with a partner. Compare your answers to **A**. If you disagree,*
discuss why you answered as you did. If you cannot come to an
agreement, check your answers in a dictionary.

C. *On a sheet of paper, classify the words in **A** according to meaning.*
Write the names of your categories here. Then explain why you think
these words were borrowed from other languages.

_____

_____

_____

 ## PRACTICE 6:
Could You Go Over
That Again, Please?

Work with a partner. One partner
*looks at **A**. The other partner*
*looks at **B** on page 48. Share*
your information using the
language for asking for
clarification and for defining.

Part A
1. You are reading an article about animation, and you come
across the term **married print.** Ask your friend, who has
written a research report on animation, what this term means.
2. You have taken a course in film editing. You know that the
term **dissolve** refers to an editorial device in which a second
shot, or picture, is allowed to emerge through a first and
replace it on the screen.

PRACTICE 7:
Haven't You Had Enough?

A. Reread "Creating Life" on pages 42–43 and underline all the examples of the present perfect tense. What meaning of the present perfect is being used in each case? Mark each item with a letter described in **B.**

B. Read each sentence and identify the meaning of the present perfect tense. Write **U** for an activity that happened or didn't happen at an unspecified time in the past, **R** for an activity that repeated, or **C** for an activity that started in the past and is continuing in the present.

_____ **1.** I haven't ever seen a worse movie!

_____ **2.** I've had enough of these violent movies! Let's go see a comedy.

_____ **3.** She has taken a number of marvelous underwater photos.

_____ **4.** This has been the best attended of any film festival in the past five years.

_____ **5.** My friend has seen *Star Wars* ten times!

_____ **6.** She's been a fan of Steven Spielberg for years.

C. What are some of your experiences with the movies? On a sheet of paper, write two sentences for each meaning of the present perfect tense. Then work with a partner and classify each other's sentences according to the instructions in **B.**

PRACTICE 8:
Parenthetical Information

A. Go back to "Creating Life" on pages 42–43 and circle the examples of parenthetical information.

B. On a sheet of paper, write a brief review of your favorite movie or of a movie you saw recently. Use at least three examples of parenthetical expressions.

PRACTICE 9:
Omnimax

A. How have movie theaters been transformed to accommodate new film technologies? What did the first theaters look like? How are modern theaters different? Share your ideas with the class.

B. Listen to the presentation about Omnimax theaters. Label each statement as true **(T)** or false **(F).**

_____ **1.** The Omnimax screen is flat and wide.

_____ **2.** An Omnimax theater is arranged like a planetarium.

_____ **3.** There are eleven speakers in an Omnimax theater.

_____ **4.** The photographic film used for an Omnimax presentation is wider than normal movie film.

_____ **5.** Special cameras are needed to photograph the images.

_____ **6.** The sound track is not on the film as in a normal movie; it's played on another machine.

_____ **7.** Sprockets are the holes the film runs over.

_____ **8.** There are nineteen Omnimax theaters in the United States.

_____ **9.** An Omnimax movie uses special effects similar to those in *Star Wars.*

_____ **10.** It's always best to sit toward the back of an Omnimax theater.

PRACTICE 10:
D *Is for Disaster*

Underline the pairs of letters that represent the sounds that should be reduced and held in these sentences. Some sentences contain more than one pair. When you have finished, listen and check your predictions. Then say the sentences with a partner.

1. Disaster movies such as *The Towering Inferno* and *Earthquake* captivated delighted film goers in the early 1970s.

2. The catastrophe at the center of such movies was always shown in gruesome, horrid detail.

3. The disaster revealed both the worst and best in human nature.

4. The object of the disaster was always one of humankind's proudest technological achievements—an unsinkable ocean liner, a fireproof skyscraper, or a jumbo jet.

5. It's interesting to note that these films were favored during a "back to nature" movement in America.

6. These movies showed how Mother Nature can unleash her powers— tidal waves, lightning, and earthquakes—to fight back at the exploitative technological advancement of modern society.

PRACTICE 11:
Organizational Patterns

A. *What is the main idea of "Creating Life" (pages 42–43)? Is the conclusion the same as the main idea? If not, what is the conclusion? Compare your ideas to a partner's.*

B. *In the space below, draw a diagram or write a description of the organizational pattern of "Creating Life."*

PRACTICE 12:
I'm Confused!

A. *Read the partial conversations. Underline the language of indicating confusion and circle the language of repairing communication.*

Conversation A

MARIAN: OK, now that the project has been explained, let's get down to business.

MITCHELL: Wait a minute. I think I must have missed something. I'm not sure who's supposed to do what.

MARIAN: Oh, I thought I'd told you. I must have lost my train of thought.

Conversation B

PETER: Have I misunderstood you? I thought you said that Anne would be in charge of photography.

YOKO: What I'm trying to say is that Anne will be in charge of the still photography, but Federico is in charge of the action shots like always.

Conversation C

JANE: Actually, that's not what I said. I think a candid shot would be better than a portrait.

KEVIN: But I thought the whole point was that we wanted more formality.

JANE: No, we want just the reverse. Formality is out. Spontaneity is in.

B. *Work with a partner. Choose one of the partial conversations and expand on it. You can add sections to the beginning, the end, or both.*

PRACTICE 13:
The Source of the Citation

These are quotations you copied down for an essay on moviemaking. On a sheet of paper, write a paraphrase of each quote and cite it according to the convention given.

1. Paraphrase: Author Not Mentioned in Sentence

Schechter, Harold and David Everitt. *Film Tricks: Special Effects in the Movies,* page 39. New York: Harlin Quist Book, 1980.

"Although D. W. Griffith made enormous contributions to the development of the movies, he is not a particularly important figure in the history of special effects, since he shied away from using them, apparently believing that they were a form of cinematic cheating."

2. Paraphrase: Author Mentioned in Text

Whitaker, Rod. *The Language of Film,* page 173. Englewood Cliffs, NJ: Prentice-Hall Inc., 1970.

"Regardless of the plastic used to record the message, regardless of the distribution and viewing circumstances, it will be the kind of visual personality we now identify as the filmmaker—not the audiovisual businessman we know as the television producer—who will create tomorrow's visual expression."

A. Grammar

*Read the conversation. Classify which meaning of the present perfect is used in each case. Write **U** for an activity that happened or didn't happen at an unspecified time in the past, **R** for an activity that repeated, or **C** for an action that started in the past and is continuing in the present.*

MIKE: Sonya, have you ever heard about "virtual reality"? (**1.** _____)

SONYA: Yeah, I've heard about it a couple of times this week.
(**2.** _____) It's a hot topic of conversation.

MIKE: I don't really understand what it is. Can you shed some light?

SONYA: Well, even though I've been interested in the graphic capability of computers for some time now, (**3.** _____) I really haven't looked into this in depth yet. (**4.** _____) I know it's supposed to give you the illusion that you're really experiencing some simulated event. And I know that it's been in development for about fifteen years (**5.** _____) and in actual use for about six.

MIKE: OK, but who uses it?

SONYA: So far, it's been used mainly for training military helicopter pilots and in video arcade games. (**6.** _____)

MIKE: Oh, I think I've seen it in an arcade down the street.
(**7.** _____) In fact, now that I think of it, it has become very popular. (**8.** _____) Where do you think it will be used in the future?

SONYA: I understand that it will be quite useful in all types of simulation training, in the field of medicine, and in the entertainment and film industry.

B. Reading and Writing

In Unit 4, you read about translating from one language to another—that in some ways translations work well, but in other ways translations can never succeed. Do you think books can be adequately translated into movies? Think of a movie you've seen that was based on a book you've read. Do you think some things were done better in the book? in the movie? Why do you think there are few examples of original movies being turned into books? Write a short essay explaining your ideas. Follow the steps of the writing process. Then file your final version in your writing portfolio.

Part B for Practice 6

1. You have just completed a research report on animation. You know that the final print of the film for a movie, which carries both the picture and the sound track, is called the **married print.**

2. You are reading an article about film editing and you come across the term **dissolve.** Ask your friend, who has taken a course in film editing, what this means.

UNIT 7 The Job for You!

PRACTICE 1:
Map Out a Job

Finding a job is an important step in anyone's life. Complete the word map with words and phrases associated with finding a job.

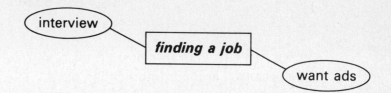

interview — finding a job — want ads

PRACTICE 2:
An Ideal Job

A. Have you ever had a job? If you've had more than one, which was your favorite? How did you get it? Did it take you a long time to find it? What steps did you go through to get hired? In what ways was this an ideal job for you? In what ways was it not ideal? Share your experiences with a partner.

B. In addition to deciding whether a job is right for you, you must decide if you are right for the job. You must ask yourself what your strengths, weaknesses, likes, and dislikes are and determine whether they are appropriate for your chosen career. Write your chosen career on the line. Then list from three to five characteristics you think people who enter that field should have. You can choose words from this list or use ideas of your own.

adaptable	dependable	perceptive
analytical	detail-oriented	pleasant
conscientious	efficient	realistic
cooperative	extroverted	supportive
creative	independent	
decisive	organized	

My chosen career: _____

Characteristics: _____

C. Work with a partner. Explain why you think someone in your chosen career should have the characteristics you named. Tell your partner whether you have these characteristics. Give examples to justify your thinking.

PRACTICE 3:
A Resume

A resume introduces you to a prospective employer by giving a summary of your professional qualifications. Read the resume on page 50; then read the explanation and answer the questions on page 51.

Josephine LeBon
1458 S. Main Street
Chicago, IL 60614
(312) 555-6930

OBJECTIVE: To find an editorial position in which I can use my organizational and communication skills.

ACCOMPLISHMENTS:

Writing/Editing

Summer intern in classifieds department of the Chicago Sun Standard, June–September, 1992. Answered phone and helped customers write and edit classified ads.

Features Editor of the Southtown High School Bugle, 1991–1992. Chose and edited articles for the features page of monthly high-school newspaper.

Organizing/Communications

Spring Dance Refreshments Committee Chairperson, May, 1990. Organized the choosing, purchasing, and serving of refreshments for annual Spring Dance.

Buena Vista Playground Supervisor, Summer, 1989. Oversaw games program for seven- to ten-year-olds at large city playground.

Freshman Class Student Council Member, 1988–1989. Participated in all aspects of student government.

EDUCATION:

Southtown High School, Chicago, IL 60614. Graduated with honors, 1992.

AWARDS:

Spanish Teachers' Association Outstanding Student, March, 1991

District Sixteen 1989 Student Government Essay Contest, Fourth Place

WORK HISTORY:

Chicago Sun Standard, June–September, 1992
Lou's Sandwich Shop, June–September, 1991, June–September, 1990
Buena Vista Playground, June–September, 1989

A. *There are two basic kinds of resumes—chronological and functional. A chronological resume lists and describes all the jobs a person has held in reverse chronological order. A functional resume lists and describes any experience a person has had that could be related to the job he or she seeks.*

1. What kind of resume did Josephine LeBon write?

_____

2. Why do you think she chose to write this kind of resume?

_____

3. Imagine that you are the editor in chief of a small publishing company. You have received Josephine's resume and you are going to interview her. Write three questions you will ask her about her experience.

_____

_____

_____

B. *Work with a partner. Take turns being Josephine and an interviewer. The interviewer asks the questions he or she wrote, and Josephine answers them based on her resume.*

PRACTICE 4:
You're Repeating Yourself!

Complete each example by writing a synonym or a word-class change for each word in dark type.

1. Job-hunters shouldn't **exaggerate** on their resumes. Companies

check the information and will discover that the claims are in fact

_____ .

2. Marital status is not a qualification for a job, so an interviewer

cannot ask if you are _____ .

3. An advertisement cannot specifically ask for a man to fill a **job** if a

woman can handle the _____ just as well.

4. This position requires a lot of **decision** making. If you can't be

_____ , you had better not take the job.

5. Cooperation is the key to success in this department. A person who

can't work _____ won't last very long.

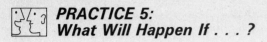

PRACTICE 5:
What Will Happen If . . . ?

A decision can have a positive or a negative result. Read each decision. Write a question about the possible outcome and two answers—one positive and one negative.

1. Your friend decides to get a part-time job in addition to his full-time job.

_____

_____

2. A classmate decides to list all of the organizations she belongs to on her resume.

_____

_____

3. Your brother decides to change careers from being a highly paid banker to being a hot-air balloon pilot.

_____

_____

4. Your aunt files a lawsuit against her company for age discrimination.

_____

_____

PRACTICE 6:
Follow the Advice!

Nina and Isabel went to a resume-writing workshop at their school's career planning department. They each got a copy of "Tips for Resume Writers." Nina followed the advice, but Isabel didn't. Write about Nina and Isabel. Use noun phrases to express cause and effect.

Because of her good organizational skills, Nina wrote an

effective resume.

1. _____

2. _____

3. _____

4. _____

5. _____

Tips For Resume Writers

1. Avoid including anything that might prove to be negative, such as a low grade-point average, political affiliation, or travel restrictions.
2. Be short and to the point.
3. Highlight your uniqueness.
4. Use action words.
5. Do not include false information.
6. Do not exaggerate accomplishments.
7. Be organized.
8. Make your resume attractive.

PRACTICE 7:
To Keep Your Job

A co-worker is giving helpful advice to a new employee at an insurance office. Fill in the blanks to make sentences that give advice.

1. To _____ , you should always show

   up on time.

2. You shouldn't make personal phone calls so as not to _____

   _____ .

3. Feel free to ask questions in order not to _____ .

4. To _____ , always be polite to the

   customers.

5. Be sure you get the customer's correct address in order to

   _____ .

Write two more pieces of advice for the new employee.

_____

_____

PRACTICE 8:
The Best Candidate for the Job

A. *Flowerdale's Department Store is going to hire an assistant store manager. Listen to the two job interviews. Fill in the chart.*

	Ms. Jenkins	Mr. Jones
Education		
Experience		
References		

B. *Listen to the interviews again. Which candidate do you think got the job? Why? Compare your answers with a partner's.*

_____

_____

_____

PRACTICE 9:
What's That Sound?

A. *Read each word and classify it according to its vowel sound.*

meet /i/	mate /e/	met /ɛ/	night /ɑɪ/
_____	_____	_____	_____
_____	_____	_____	_____
_____	_____	_____	_____
_____	_____	_____	_____

age
ease
edge
brief
buy
taste
tie
head
sheep
fail
braid
liar
leap
test

B. *Listen to the words. Check your answers and make any necessary changes in your lists.*

PRACTICE 10:
A Cover Letter

A. *Read the ad and Josephine's cover letter. Answer the questions.*

1. Look at the format of Josephine's letter.

Whose address comes first?

_____

Whose address is second?

_____

2. Look at the punctuation.

What punctuation mark is after

the greeting? _____

What punctuation mark is after

the closing? _____

3. What do you think *enc.*

means? _____

B. *Reread Gerardo's resume on page 84 of your Student Book. On a sheet of paper, write his cover letter to Snappy Shots, Inc.*

> **EDITOR WANTED**
> Hal's Happy Hamburgers seeks editor for monthly customer newsletter. Must have excellent organizational skills. Prefer some experience. Contact Hal Harwood, 1637 Clark St., Chicago, IL 60658.

1458 S. Main Street
Chicago, IL 60614
November 15, 1992

Mr. Hal Harwood
1637 Clark Street
Chicago, IL 60658

Dear Mr. Harwood:
I would like to apply for the position of editor of your monthly customer newsletter.

I believe I am very well qualified for this job. Not only do I have editorial experience, but I also worked for two summers at Lou's Sandwich Shop, so I am well acquainted with the fast food business.

I am enclosing a resume, and I look forward to hearing from you at your earliest convenience.

Sincerely,
Josephine LeBon
Josephine LeBon

enc.

PRACTICE 11:
It's Difficult to Say!

A. *In a job interview, you may be asked questions that you find stressful to answer. Read the following questions. Write responses that are well thought out but that avoid direct answers.*

1. What do you consider your two greatest weaknesses?

_____

2. Why did you leave your last job?

_____

3. Why do you think you deserve such a high salary?

_____

4. What didn't you like about your last boss?

_____

5. What's the biggest complaint anyone has ever made about you?

_____

B. *Work with a partner. Take turns asking difficult questions and avoiding giving direct answers. Use the questions from **A.***

PRACTICE 12:
Writing a Resume

A. *Reread the explanation of resumes at the top of page 51 and the "Tips for Resume Writers" on page 52.*

1. What kind of resume would you write for yourself, a chronological resume or a functional resume? Why?

_____

_____

2. Think of your accomplishments. What action words from the box could you use to describe them? List some here.

_____ _____ _____ _____ _____

_____ _____ _____ _____ _____

3. What special skills or awards would you include in your resume?

_____

_____

_____

Action Words
achieved
administered
coordinated
conceived
developed
eliminated
improved
organized
participated
proved
recommended
set up
supervised
trained
wrote

A. Grammar

Complete each sentence with words that express purpose or show cause and effect.

1. People work in order to _____ .

2. _____ so as not to get fired.

3. Due to _____ , Maria was not

interested in the job.

4. Because of _____ , Roman got the

promotion.

5. Nicolas is changing jobs to _____ .

6. As a result of _____ , Kathy is

looking for a new job.

7. So as to do well in his interview, Pedro _____

_____ .

8. Due to the recent departure of some of the employees at our

company, _____

_____ .

9. _____ in order to not seem too

aggressive.

10. _____ because of poor interpersonal

skills.

B. Reading and Writing

Most people work to gain the means for daily survival. A lucky few work because they enjoy what they do. Think about what you like doing best. What would be your ideal job if money were not an issue? Write a paragraph on a sheet of paper. Follow the steps of the writing process. Then file your paragraph in your writing portfolio.

UNIT 8 The Time of Your Life!

 PRACTICE 1:
Out of Whack

Imagine you are an astronaut on the space shuttle. List ways in which your biological clock might get out of whack.

1. _____

2. _____

3. _____

4. _____

5. _____

PRACTICE 2:
Is This Your Day?

A. *Some people believe that we have physical, emotional, and intellectual cycles, or biorhythms, that are set at birth and that by charting these cycles we can predict good and bad times in our lives. Days when a cycle switches from low to high or from high to low are thought to be ''full of danger or difficulty.'' Look at Clark Gable's biorhythm chart and answer the questions.*

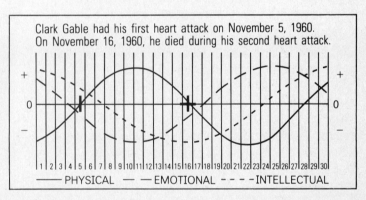

Clark Gable had his first heart attack on November 5, 1960. On November 16, 1960, he died during his second heart attack.

—— PHYSICAL — — EMOTIONAL - - - -INTELLECTUAL

1. On which days was Gable's intellectual cycle the highest?

_____

2. On which days was Gable at his lowest point emotionally?

_____

3. Gable suffered a heart attack on November 5, 1960. What do you notice about his biorhythms for that day?

_____

4. Gable died after a second heart attack on November 16. What did his biorhythms for that day show?

_____

B. *Work in a group. Answer the questions and discuss your ideas.*

1. Do you believe that patterns of behavior can be predicted at birth? Why or why not?

2. Do you think biorhythms are likely to be more or less accurate than horoscopes? Explain your reasons.

Read the article and underline the various techniques that the author uses to define words and concepts. In the margin, write the name for each technique used.

In a Dark, Silent Tank

Using sensory deprivation—in other words, restricting sensory stimulation—to enhance consciousness is not a new concept. (For example, it is well-known that blind people sometimes develop increased senses of touch and smell.) Achieving an almost perfect state of sensory deprivation has been possible since the invention of the flotation tank. A person in such a tank floats weightlessly in a saltwater solution in perfect darkness and absolute silence. Some people view these tanks as ''very Californian,'' that is, a bit crazy. But recent research by scientists, psychologists, psychiatrists, teachers, and doctors proves that there is more here than meets the eye.

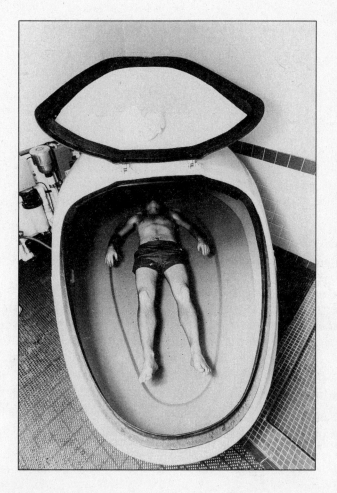

The flotation tank is the ultimate biofeedback tool, allowing the floater to become aware of his or her subtle and minute internal states and changes. The floater can reap both physiological and psychological benefits. One important outcome is the increased release of endorphins, the body's natural pain-killing substances. Research has also indicated that the use of a flotation tank can initiate weight loss and, perhaps more importantly, maintain it.

The psychological benefits of the tank are closely connected to the physical benefits. There is strong evidence that floating can help free oneself from depression, anxiety, fear, and destructive habits and addictions. In addition, one can reach an almost perfect state of relaxation and meditation. These psychological effects in turn aid the body in obtaining a general state of mental as well as physical wellness.

It has also been indicated that this type of sensory deprivation can temporarily disable the dominance of the analytical left hemisphere of the brain, permitting access to the creative, imaginative, problem-solving right hemisphere.

In summary, a variety of people might benefit from flotation for a variety of reasons. Doctors could help patients overcome stress-related illnesses such as heart disease and gastrointestinal disorders, athletes could improve performance by decreasing stress, students might successfully reduce anxiety about tests and improve learning, and artists might become more creative.

PRACTICE 4:
Idea Map

Complete the idea map for the article "In a Dark, Silent Tank." Use your finished map to tell a partner the main idea and the most important details from the article.

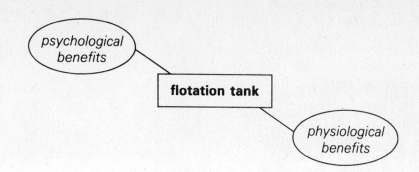

PRACTICE 5:
Do You Walk or Run a Dog?

A. Match each verb in column 1 with the appropriate noun in column 2. Write the letters on the lines.

1. deliver _____
2. place _____
3. perform _____
4. commit _____
5. draw _____

a. a crime
b. an operation
c. an order
d. a speech
e. a comparison

B. Match each numbered adjective with the appropriate noun. Write the letters on the lines. Use each word only once.

a. noise
b. climate
c. hopes
d. margin
e. error
f. headache
g. eater
h. odor
i. accent
j. interest

1. big _____
2. high _____
3. gross _____
4. warm _____
5. heavy _____

6. narrow _____
7. strong _____
8. loud _____
9. splitting _____
10. keen _____

PRACTICE 6:
Which Shift Do You Prefer?

A. Hospitals have to be in operation twenty-four hours a day, so the day is usually divided into three eight-hour shifts. A worker can work the morning, afternoon, or night shift. List some other jobs for which the day might be divided into shifts.

_____

_____

_____

B. What are the pros and cons of working each shift? Fill in the chart.

	7:00 AM to 3:00 PM	3:00 PM to 11:00 PM	11:00 PM to 7:00 AM
Pros			
Cons			

C. Work with a partner. Take turns being an employment counselor and a job hunter who is looking for one of the jobs he or she named in **A.** The job hunter should state his or her preference for working a particular shift and give reasons for the choice. The employment counselor should try to persuade the job hunter to agree to work a different shift.

Ⓖ PRACTICE 7: *Problems at Biosphere II*

Complete each sentence with a preposition and a gerund. Use information from the sentence in parentheses.

1. (Project sponsors have pumped in fresh air.)
Project sponsors of Biosphere II have been accused

_____

2. (Computers can change data about the conditions inside.)
Some critics say that Biosphere's computer programs are capable

_____

3. (Tourists shouldn't buy seedlings from the gift shop.)
Another critic says the seedlings in the gift shop were not cloned in Biosphere and warns tourists

_____

4. (A recovered worker wanted to go back to work.)
After medical treatment outside Biosphere II, one crew member was excited

_____

5. (Officials want to attract tourists.)
Biosphere II officials had said that the project was also aimed

_____

PRACTICE 8:
What's Your Stress Level?

Use the thought groups to form one logical sentence for each item.
Write your sentences on the lines.

1. one way of / reduce stress / employ biofeedback techniques

_____

2. a benefit of / regulate stress / not need to take medicine

_____

3. one solution for / relieve migraine headaches / train yourself to regulate certain body functions

_____

_____

4. a reason for / worry about stress / number of stress-related deaths increasing rapidly

_____

_____

5. the disadvantage in / think biofeedback techniques are the ultimate solution for stress management / not work for everyone

_____

_____

PRACTICE 9:
A Timely Diet

A. Fill in the column of the chart under *You*. Write **none, light, moderate,** or **heavy** for each meal. Write **yes** or **no** if you have a snack.

B. Listen to the conversation. Write the suggested diet in the chart.

C. Compare your diet with the suggested diet. Do you eat according to *The Body Clock Diet? Do you know anyone who does? Do you think this diet would really work? Could it work for you? Share your ideas with a partner.*

	You	Suggested Diet
Breakfast		
Midmorning Snack		
Lunch		
Afternoon Snack		
Dinner		
Evening Snack		

PRACTICE 10:
Odd Word Out

A. Work with a partner. Pronounce the words in each group and circle the one that does not have the same vowel sound as the others. Then listen to the words and check your answers.

1. clown	pouch	mow	drown
2. thought	float	devote	owner
3. caller	flawed	broad	load
4. shoe	below	pool	jewel
5. draw	point	employer	joyous

B. Make up five similar examples of your own and exchange them with your partner. Find your partner's odd words out.

PRACTICE 11:
Mnemonics

A. Look back at the suggested Body Clock Diet in Practice 9 on page 61. Think of a mnemonic strategy to help you remember what to eat when. Your device can be letter associations, visual associations, or whatever will help you remember the diet. Write your strategy on a sheet of paper.

B. Compare your strategy with a partner's. How are your strategies different? Without looking back at page 61, explain the diet to your partner by using your mnemonic strategy.

PRACTICE 12:
Proposing and Analyzing Solutions

A. Read the problems. Write a solution for each.

1. You are the manager of a factory that operates twenty-four hours a day in three eight-hour shifts. How can you divide the shifts fairly among the employees? How can you help them cope?

_____

2. You and your spouse are suffering from asynchronous circadian rhythms (mismatched sleep-wake cycles). How can you get in sync?

_____

3. You have a newborn baby. Neither you nor your spouse can sleep. You are getting very cranky with each other. What can you do?

_____

B. Work with a partner. Take turns proposing your solutions to the problems and analyzing those solutions.

PRACTICE 13:
Choosing and Narrowing a Topic

You are going to write an essay on a topic related to biological clocks. Think about what you have learned in this unit and go through these steps.

1. Here are some ideas for topics. Add four or five ideas of your own.

animal hibernation
the effect of diet on biological clocks _____
sleep-wake cycles of astronauts
morning people and night people _____

_____

_____

2. Choose one of the ideas in **1** as the topic of your essay. What resources will you use to find out more about the topic? List at least three.

_____

_____

_____

3. What prewriting and organizing strategies will you use to generate and organize the ideas in your essay? List at least three.

_____

_____

_____

4. Choose one of the strategies from **3** and develop it here. You might brainstorm some ideas; make an idea map, time line, or cube; or jot down some questions for your research.

5. Use the information from **4** as well as from any research you have done and write a rough draft of your essay.
6. Show your essay to a partner to check for content, clarity, and organization. Then write your final version.

A. Grammar

Complete the paragraph by writing an appropriate preposition or gerund in each blank.

Many hospitals require employees to rotate shifts. For some employees,

it is hard to get used **(1)** _____ **(2. change)** _____

their schedules every week. Some hospitals have become concerned

(3) _____ **(4. rotate)** _____ workers between day and

night shifts because workers whose shifts are rotated are more likely to

be involved in accidents on the job. One study has shown that a way

(5) _____ **(6. help)** _____ night-shift workers adapt is

(7) _____ **(8. assign)** _____ them to successively

later shifts rather than to earlier shifts. Shifts should also be rotated

every three weeks instead of every week. These measures help ensure

alert workers in safe workplaces.

B. Reading and Writing

Think about a time when your biological clock went out of whack. What caused the problem? How long did the problem last? How did it affect your life? What did you do, if anything, to relieve the problem? Write an essay describing what happened. Analyze the problem and tell how you might prevent it from occurring again in the future. Remember to follow the steps of the writing process. When you are finished, file your essay in your writing portfolio.

PRACTICE 1:
Continental Drift

Many earthquakes and volcanoes are caused by the movement of the earth's tectonic plates. Each of the continents is the top of a tectonic plate. Other plates lie under the oceans. The plates covered by land are heavier and move much more slowly than the ones covered by water. The African plate, for example, hasn't moved very far in about thirty million years. The Pacific plate, on the other hand, moves northwest about five inches a year. As it moves, it grinds against the North American plate, building up pressure until it causes an earthquake. During the San Francisco earthquake of 1906, the Pacific plate moved an incredible twenty feet in less than a minute!

Study the map. What predictions can you make about the future? Write a list.

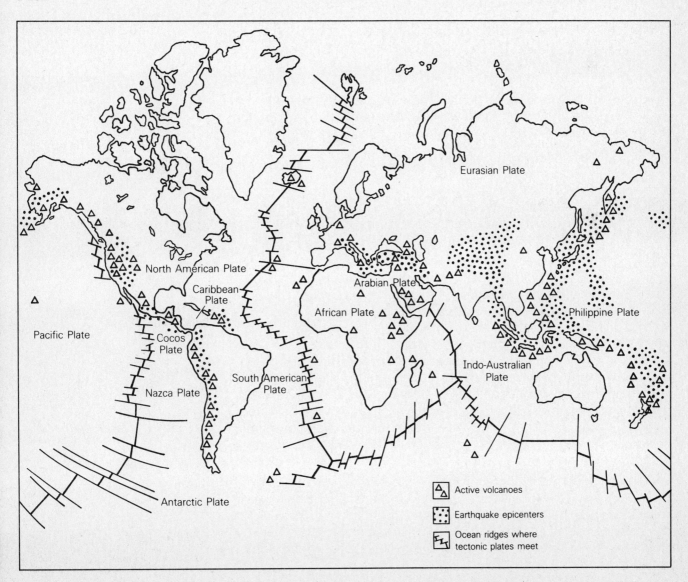

Eurasian Plate

North American Plate

Caribbean Plate

Arabian Plate

African Plate

Philippine Plate

Pacific Plate

Cocos Plate

Indo-Australian Plate

Nazca Plate

South American Plate

Antarctic Plate

△△ Active volcanoes

⋮⋮ Earthquake epicenters

Ocean ridges where tectonic plates meet

 **PRACTICE 2:**
Volcano

A. *What do you associate with the term* **volcano?** *Make an idea map.*

<pre>
┌─────────────┐
│   volcano   │
└─────────────┘
</pre>

B. *Compare your idea map with that of a partner. How are the idea maps similar? different? With your partner, list things you would like to know about volcanoes.*

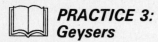 **PRACTICE 3:**
Geysers

Have you ever seen a geyser? Do you know what causes geysers? Read "Eruptions of Water." Then draw and label a diagram of a geyser on a sheet of paper.

Eruptions of Water

A geyser is a spring from which hot water, steam, or mud gushes out at intervals, frequently to a considerable height. This type of hot-spot eruption is similar to a volcano's except that a volcano spews out molten rock instead of water.

Geysers occur in places where water drains deep into the earth. A deep channel cuts down from the surface into the interior, often with horizontal channels connected to it. Cold water seeps through these channels until, deep below the surface, it reaches very hot rocks, warmed either by the natural heat of the earth's interior or by magma, the molten material beneath the earth's crust. The rocks heat the water and, as the temperature of the water at the bottom of the channel reaches 100 degrees Celsius, bubbles of steam form. The bubbles rise, pushing up the cooler water above and spilling some of it out of the opening and onto the surface. This makes the column of water lighter, and more water is able to turn into steam. This in turn lifts the column more, until suddenly the rest of the water turns to steam, exploding upward. As the water and steam fall back to earth, they cool and begin to seep back down to fill up the channel, and the process begins again.

Each geyser differs in its frequency and in the length and height of its explosion. Old Faithful in Yellowstone National Park is perhaps the most famous due to its regularity of explosion—approximately every thirty to ninety minutes, lasting two to five minutes, and reaching fifty meters into the air.

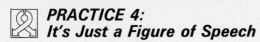

PRACTICE 4:
It's Just a Figure of Speech

Similes and hyperboles are often used in ordinary speech to help emphasize the speaker's feelings. Complete each simile or hyperbole with an idea of your own.

1. The noise of the volcano was so loud that _____

_____

2. I was so frightened that _____

3. After the eruption, the land looked as if _____

_____

4. The water was as hot as _____

5. The sunset was like _____

PRACTICE 5:
Let's Get Out of Here!

You and your friend live near a volcano that many scientists feel is going to erupt at any minute. With a partner, take turns playing Friend A and Friend B. Use the facts and examples in the boxes to convince your partner to take the viewpoint of the friend you are playing.

Friend A
You have lived near this volcano all your life. There have been several times in the past when you felt small tremors, and there have been several winters when the snow on the mountain melted, but nothing serious has ever happened. You think it's foolish to worry, and you don't intend to leave your home. Try to convince your friend to stay too.

Friend B
You are very worried about the volcano and think everyone should evacuate the area. Use these facts to try to convince your friend to leave.
1. Scientists have recorded three seismic tremors from inside the volcano in the last twenty-four hours. This is a good indicator of an impending blast.
2. Chemical sensors have detected increased amounts of sulfur-dioxide emissions. This is evidence that magma has neared the surface.
3. Laser-based devices have detected that the north side of the volcano has swollen. This is exactly what happened before the eruption of Mount St. Helens.
4. The snow on top of the mountain is melting. This is another sign that hot magma is near the surface.

PRACTICE 6:
Mount St. Helens

Mount St. Helens erupted with incredible violence on the morning of May 18, 1980. Put the words in each noun phrase in order. Complete each sentence with the correct noun phrase.

a. population   nearly   the   of   all   waterfowl
b. earthquake   a   severe   truly
c. extensive   extremely   the   ashfall
d. most   the   experiences   one   horrifying   of
e. sophisticated   most   one   facilities   of   the

1. People described the eruption as _____

_____ in their lives.

2. The eruption may have been caused by _____

_____ that measured five on the

Richter scale.

3. _____ in the world for

volcano research is located at the University of Washington.

4. _____ damaged much

of the ecology of the area.

5. _____ was wiped out

by the explosion.

PRACTICE 7:
Please Come to Order

Put the words in each noun phrase in order. Then use each phrase in a sentence. Write the sentence on the line.

a. compact   an   laser   incredibly   printer
b. new   most   of   video   the   innovative   programs   the
c. sauce   Mexican   very   the   spicy   taco
d. scissors   left-handed   orange-handled   the
e. global   the   important   first   treaty

1. _____

2. _____

3. _____

4. _____

5. _____

UNIT 9   HOT SPOTS

PRACTICE 8:
Interview with a Volcanologist

A. *Listen to the interview and answer the questions.*

1. What do volcanologists do?

_____

2. What do volcanologists hope to learn?

_____

3. How are shield volcanoes formed?

_____

_____

4. How are stratovolcanoes formed?

_____

_____

B. *Would you like to be a volcanologist? What would you like about the job? dislike about it? Write your ideas on the lines. Then share them with a partner.*

_____

_____

_____

_____

PRACTICE 9:
Thought Groups

Divide each sentence into thought groups and mark them with slashes. Then, with a partner, take turns reading the sentences, paying special attention to the division of the groups and the rhythm. Finally, listen to the sentences to check your work.

1. A hot spring is a flow of water that is heated by forces within the earth and that surfaces naturally from the ground.
2. The water can contain salts and minerals that people feel are beneficial to health.
3. Not surprisingly, these hot springs have become commercialized and are popular destinations for vacations and treatments.
4. There are famous hot spring spas and resorts in England, Argentina, Germany, and the United States.

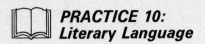

PRACTICE 10:
Literary Language

A. *Literary language is most often used in poetry. Alfred, Lord Tennyson (1809–1892) was an English poet. Read each quote from Tennyson's poetry and tell if it contains* **alliteration, onomatopoeia,** *or* **repetition.**

1. Break, break, break,

On thy cold gray stones, O Sea! _____

2. He clasps the crag with crooked hands; _____

3. A gown of grass-green silk she wore, _____

4. And the clash and boom of the bells rang into the heart and the

brain. _____

B. *Read each of these quotes from Tennyson and tell if it contains* **simile, personification, metaphor,** *or* **hyperbole.**

1. Cold upon the dead volcano sleeps the gleam of dying day.

_____

2. Eager-hearted as a boy when first he leaves

His father's field. _____

3. So like a painted battle the war stood Silenced. _____

4. . . . the world was so clear about him that he saw the smallest rock

far on the faintest hill, _____

PRACTICE 11:
Providing Support

A. *You are a developmental editor for a new book of readings for students who are learning English. Your boss has asked you to bring ideas for unit themes to the next meeting. Write down some ideas.*

_____

_____

B. *Work in a group. As members of the editorial team for the new book of readings, your job is to decide on six unit themes that are useful, interesting, relevant, or that meet any other criteria you choose. Be sure to use language for providing support for other group members. Write the six themes your group chooses.*

_____

_____

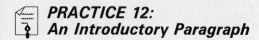

PRACTICE 12:
An Introductory Paragraph

This is the introductory paragraph to a chapter about Mount Vesuvius in a book on volcanoes. Read the paragraph and answer the questions.

Shadows over the Cradle of Man

By any measure of geologic time, Mount Vesuvius is but an infant among earth features, and as a volcano it is unremarkable in a number of respects. The mountain is scarcely 17,000 years old and stands only 4,200 feet above Italy's Bay of Naples. And yet this relatively minor mountain is the most celebrated of volcanoes. It has been intimately involved with mankind for at least 3,000 years and is surrounded by the largest population—two million people—ever to dwell in the immediate vicinity of an active crater. No other volcano has played so definitive a role in history, or has so dramatized the perils and benefactions that are visited upon those who choose to live along the flanks of an eruptive peak.

1. Where is the thesis statement in this paragraph? Is this the most effective place for it? Why or why not?

_____

_____

2. Which sentence in the paragraph provides examples to clarify a previous sentence?

_____

3. Which sentence in the paragraph offers a contrast to previous information?

_____

4. What audience do you think the writer had in mind? How do you know?

_____

PRACTICE 13:
Writing an Introduction

A. *You are going to write an essay about tapping geothermal energy as an alternative to using fossil fuels (coal and oil). Who will be the audience for your essay? What kind of information will you need to put in your introductory paragraph?*

B. *Research the topic and write an introductory paragraph on a sheet of paper. Show your paragraph to a partner to check for content, clarity, and organization. Rewrite the paragraph, and then complete the essay.*

A. Grammar

Put the words in each noun phrase in order. Then use the phrase in a sentence. Write the sentence on the lines.

1. shoes   of   wooden   traditional   most   Dutch   the

_____

_____

2. his   incredibly   account   firsthand   fascinating

_____

_____

3. figures   miniature   the   of   Peruvian   gold   some

_____

_____

4. ceremonial   beautiful   masks   white   several   Kabuki

_____

_____

5. Russian   boxes   lacquer   one   the   finest   of   circular

_____

_____

B. Reading and Writing

What natural disasters can occur in the area of the world where you live? (volcanic eruptions? earthquakes? floods? tornadoes? hurricanes?) Write a short essay describing the kind of disaster that can happen and give information on what you would do to survive the disaster. Be persuasive so your readers will follow your advice. When you are finished, file your essay in your writing portfolio.

PRACTICE 1:
Punning Around

A pun is a play on words—the humorous use of a word that has different meanings or of two or more words that have different meanings but that sound the same or almost the same. Write the words or meanings that each of these puns confuses.

1. A doctor should always keep his temper because he can't afford to lose his patients.

_____

2. An egotist is someone who is always me-deep in conversation.

_____

3. The butcher put a lot of bread in the sausages because she couldn't make both ends meat.

_____

4. Why is a dog's tail like the center of a tree? Because it's the farthest from the bark.

_____

 PRACTICE 2:
Poking Fun

A. *Humorists often poke fun at human behavior or attitudes. What is the cartoonist poking fun at in each of these cartoons?*

BABY BLUES by Jerry Scott and Rick Kirkman
By permission of Jerry Scott, Rick Kirkman and Creators Syndicate

"DO YOU WISH TO ORDER NOW, OR DO YOU NEED SOME MORE TIME TO ADD UP THE CALORIES?"

B. *Choose your favorite cartoon on this page. Is the cartoonist poking fun at a behavior or attitude that is specific to one culture or that is universal?*

What do you have to know in order to get the joke? Write your ideas. Then share them with a partner.

_____

_____

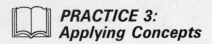

PRACTICE 3:
Applying Concepts

Understanding humor often depends on applying what you know. As you read the jokes, think about what the writer assumes the reader knows. Make inferences about anything you don't know for sure.

My friend Roberta came up with a perfect solution to her garbage problem during a recent strike of the garbage workers in New York City. Every morning she would wrap up her garbage in beautiful gift paper and put the package in a Gucci shopping bag. When she went to work, she'd park her car on the street with the window open and the bag sitting on the front seat. When she got back to the car at night, the garbage was always gone.

A guy I went to school with joined a computer dating service. He told the computer he was looking for someone short who likes crowds, enjoys water sports, and is happy wearing formal clothes. The computer fixed him up with a penguin.

When my cousin Fred filled out a job application at Apple Computer, he wrote this as his qualifications: "I graduated first in my class at MIT. I turned down a vice-presidency at IBM. Money means nothing to me, so I don't care what my salary is. And I'm willing to work sixty hours a week."

"My goodness!" said the job interviewer. "Don't you have any weaknesses?"

"Well," said Fred, "I'll have to admit that I do tell lies."

1. Have you ever heard of Gucci's? What can you infer from the first joke? Write your answer; then check page 75.

_____

2. Do you know what MIT stands for? what IBM stands for? What can you infer about these two places from the third joke? Write your answer; then check page 75.

_____

3. What behavior or attitude does the first joke poke fun at? Is this behavior or attitude specific to one culture, or is it universal? Give reasons for your answer.

_____

_____

4. What behavior or attitude does the second joke poke fun at? Is this behavior or attitude specific to one culture, or is it universal? Give reasons for your answer.

_____

_____

PRACTICE 4:
Lexically Speaking

A. Read the list of words. Divide them into three lexical sets and label each set. Add two words of your own to each set.

ambiguous	fresh	ocean	stuffy
clean	hemisphere	poem	subtropical
cold	idiom	rain forest	synonym
context	nose	sense	universal
cultivate	nostril	smoky	weather
fertile			

idiom	fresh	ocean

B. Compare your sets with a partner's. Did you put the same words in each set? If there are differences, how do you explain them?

PRACTICE 5:
Association Game

A. In two minutes, write in the space below as many words as you can think of that you associate with the word **health.**

**Information for
Practice 3: Applying Concepts**
Gucci's is a chain of exclusive shops that sells very expensive leather goods and other fashions and accessories.
MIT (the Massachusetts Institute of Technology) is a famous school of engineering and other sciences.
IBM (International Business Machines) is one of the world's largest manufacturers of computers and software.

B. Work with a group. Take turns reading your words aloud. As each word is read, everyone who wrote that word must cross it out. The person with the most words not crossed out wins.

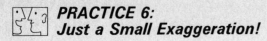

PRACTICE 6:
Just a Small Exaggeration!

A. *Texas is the largest of the forty-eight contiguous states, and there are many jokes about the fact that everything is big in Texas. Read the jokes. Then make up your own exaggerations about a swimming pool, a skyscraper, and being rich.*

1. A Texas family's swimming pool is so large it has high and low tides.

_____

2. A new Texas skyscraper is so tall that the elevators show movies.

_____

3. A Texas couple is so rich that their son's piggy bank has two vice-presidents and a guard.

_____

B. *Work with a partner. Make a short conversation using each of these exaggerations.*

1. The baby started to scream like a fire siren!
2. The mosquitoes were as big as helicopters!
3. There were about a million people crammed into one small room.

PRACTICE 7:
A Few of My Favorite Things

Combine the nouns in each item to make a genitive. Use the genitive as the subject of a sentence about yourself.

1. title/favorite movie

_____

2. best friend/favorite hobby

_____

3. mother/favorite color

_____

4. author/favorite book

_____

5. favorite brand/soft drink

_____

PRACTICE 8:
The Point of the Joke

Complete each item with the appropriate form of the genitive.

The symphony conductor was rehearsing the second movement

(1) _____ Beethoven **(2)** _____ Ninth Symphony when the

violinist **(3)** _____ cat meowed. The conductor threw down his baton

and shouted, "Would the owner **(4)** _____ that cat please take it out

and have it tuned!"

Ms. Smith **(5)** _____ dance class was rehearsing Stravinsky **(6)** _____

"The Rite **(7)** _____ Spring." One of the dancers was way out of step.

"What's the matter?" asked Ms. Smith. "Can't you hear the rhythm

(8) _____ the music?" "Oh, sure," replied the student. "But I don't

let it bother me."

PRACTICE 9:
You Want to Be a What?

A. *Do you and your parents agree about your choice of career? How might your parents have reacted if you had chosen a career such as wild animal training or skydiving? List some advice you have received about choosing a career.*

_____

_____

_____

B. *Steve Calechman is a young stand-up comic. Listen to how he describes his mother's reaction to his choice of career. List at least three ways Steve's mother lets him know how she feels about his choice.*

_____

_____

_____

C. *How much influence do you think parents should have on their children's choice of careers? Why do you feel as you do? Share your opinions with a partner. Do you agree?*

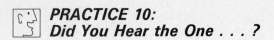

PRACTICE 10:
Did You Hear the One . . . ?

A. *Read the following joke and underline the stressed syllables. Then listen to the joke and check your answers.*

A: Have you heard the one about the psychiatrists and the light bulb?

B: No, how does it go?

A: How many psychiatrists does it take to change a light bulb?

B: I have no idea. How many does it take?

A: Only one, but the light bulb has really got to want to change.

B. *Read the joke aloud to a partner. Be sure to link or reduce the function words and pronouns between the stressed words. When you are finished, switch roles.*

PRACTICE 11:
The Right Audience

A. *Fill in the chart about five TV shows you watched in the last week.*

Name of Show	Intended Audience

B. *Do you fit the profile of the intended audience for all five of the shows you watched? Choose one show for which you were probably not the intended audience and tell why you watched it.*

_____

_____

_____

_____

_____

_____

_____

_____

PRACTICE 12:
Smile, You're on Candid Camera!

A. *Work in a group. You are situation writers for Candid Camera. You must come up with two new situations to catch people in. Be sure to keep the discussion on topic when participants digress. Write your group's situations here.*

_____

_____

B. *Combine your group with another or work as a class. You must choose three situations for this week's TV show. Defend your group's ideas and try to persuade everyone to choose them.*

PRACTICE 13:
What's Your Opinion?

A. *What do you think humor is? Do you agree with any of these statements?*

The secret source of humor . . . is not joy but sorrow.
Mark Twain

Good taste and humor are a contradiction in terms . . .
Malcolm Muggeridge

Humor is falling downstairs, if you do it in the act of warning your wife not to.
Kenneth Bird

Humor is merely tragedy standing on its head with its pants torn.
Irvin S. Cobb

Malcom
Muggeridge

Mark Twain

B. *Make an idea map for **humor.***

humor

C. *Use your ideas from **B** to write an essay giving your views on humor. Be sure to give examples, explanations, and so on, to support your opinions.*

A. Grammar

Complete each item with the appropriate form of the genitive.

In the professor **(1)** _____ last lecture **(2)** _____ the term, she

emphasized that the students **(3)** _____ time should be devoted to

preparing for the final exam. "The examinations are now in the hands

(4) _____ the typist," she said. "Are there any questions?"

"Yes," said a voice. "What's the typist **(5)** _____ name?"

The parents **(6)** _____ a boy who had just gotten his driver **(7)** _____

license were upset because the boy always wanted to use his

father **(8)** _____ car. He even wanted to drive to the home **(9)** _____

a friend who lived only two blocks away. "You have two good feet,"

said the boy **(10)** _____ mother. "What do you think they're for?"

"The gas and the brake!" the boy replied.

B. Reading and Writing

What kind of humor do you like most? Do your friends agree with you about what's funny? Survey five or six close friends about the kind of humor they like most. Then write a short essay giving your opinion about the importance of friends' sharing a sense of humor. Use examples from your survey to support your position. Follow the steps of the writing process. Then file your essay in your writing portfolio.

PRACTICE 1:
Culture Map

A. What elements do you think make up a culture? Complete the idea map.

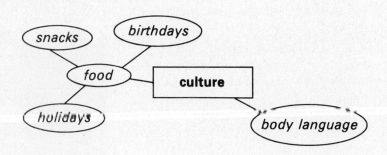

B. Compare your map with a partner's. Did you include the same elements? If you and your partner included different elements, discuss them and agree to add them to or delete them from both maps.

 PRACTICE 2:
Who's Uncivilized?

A. People of all cultures have an attitude of "us" versus "them." "Us" is equated with polite, intelligent, and civilized behavior; whereas "them" is sometimes viewed as rough, crude, and uncivilized. Take, for example, the reactions of the Yanomamo Indians of the Amazon jungle when the first outsiders, a group of highly educated American scientists, visited their home. The Yanomamo found the Americans to be weak, pitiful creatures who couldn't use bows and arrows and who couldn't deal with the mosquitoes. Another example, is the Japanese, who clean themselves before sitting in a bathtub and find it uncivilized that westerners sit in their own dirty bath water.

What do you consider uncivilized behavior? Are there aspects of your culture that others might consider uncivilized? Share your ideas.

B. You are a visitor from outer space. List at least five things that earthlings do that you find quite uncivilized. (Be creative!)

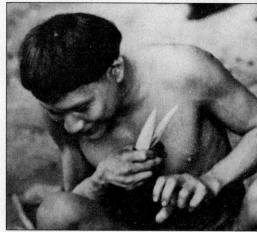

Yanomamo Indian

_____

_____

_____

_____

_____

PRACTICE 3:
Descriptions

A. *Read the article "For My Daughter," paying attention to the descriptive language. Fill in the chart on page 83 with the author's impressions of each city.*

For My Daughter

I have become a world traveler, pretty much at home wherever I go. So when you asked me to reminisce about my first trip abroad, I was surprised to pull from my memory the images of being "a stranger in a strange land." I am writing this down so it can become part of our family history—so it won't be lost.

Most of my life had been spent in the Midwest—growing up in a small city in Michigan, going on vacations in Wisconsin, visiting relatives and shopping in Chicago, studying at the University of Michigan. I had liked staying near home. However, things changed while I was studying Russian at the university. I was going to study for a semester in Leningrad, as St. Petersburg was then called, and I decided to prepare myself by spending the summer working with Russian immigrants in Boston.

St. Petersburg

To me, being in Boston was a bit like traveling abroad. The Boston accent sounded "funny" to my midwestern ears. Traffic seemed much worse than at home. Even the look of the city was different from what I was used to. Although there were some modern skyscrapers like those in Chicago, many buildings in Boston had been built before Chicago was founded! The orderliness of Chicago streets was missing too—instead of being wide and straight, the streets in Boston were narrow and followed crooked old cow paths. But I reveled in the differences. It was exciting!

Soon the summer ended, and I began my first trip abroad. I arrived in Russia in September. I remember that even though the sun was shining, the modern concrete buildings looked cold and gray. The historic buildings, on the other hand, were amazingly beautiful from afar—I felt as if I might run into Peter the Great. But up close you could see that the paint was peeling and the structures were crumbling.

Chicago

My student dormitory was very different from the dormitories at the University of Michigan. It wasn't very well lit, and the dimness and the extremely high ceilings gave me the feeling of being in a cave. Student food was not what I was used to either, as it consisted mainly of thick cabbage soup and dark bread.

In my free time, I loved strolling along the wide, tree-lined boulevard next to the river, but I felt a little out of place. My clothing (a bright-colored parka and blue jeans) was like a beacon that flashed "foreigner, foreigner, foreigner." People weren't used to seeing many Americans and, although they were friendly, their stares and whispers as I walked by disconcerted me.

So, although I wouldn't have missed the experience for the world, one thing is sure—after four months I was ready to go home to the purple mountain majesties and amber waves of grain!

---

82   **UNIT 11   FAR AND WIDE**

	Streets	Food	Buildings
Boston			
St. Petersburg			

B. *Why do you think the author did not describe the food in Boston?*

_____

 PRACTICE 4:
What Are You Referring To?

A. *In "For My Daughter," the author quotes the title of a book (Stranger in a Strange Land) and some song lyrics ("purple mountain majesties," and "amber waves of grain" from the song "America the Beautiful"). Are you familiar with either of these works? Write your answers about them on the lines.*

1. What ideas come to your mind from the title *Stranger in a Strange Land?*

_____

2. What ideas come to your mind from the song lyrics?

_____

B. *Read about these works on page 87. What other ideas come to your mind after reading this information? Why do you think the author quoted these particular works? Share your thoughts with a partner.*

 PRACTICE 5:
Descriptive Language

Choose a medium from column 1 and a topic from column 2. Write a descriptive paragraph in the medium you chose on a sheet of paper. Appeal to as many of the senses as possible.

1. your school newspaper
a local newspaper
a letter to a friend
a letter to your parents
a national magazine
your own idea

2. an accident
an open-air market
a recent party
a local festival
a nearby historical monument
your own idea

PRACTICE 6:
Expressing Anger and Resolving Conflict

A. *You are on a driving trip across the United States. It's a little after ten o'clock at night when you arrive in a small town and find a room at a motel. In your culture, dinner is usually eaten between nine o'clock and midnight, so you're hungry. The owner of the motel directs you to a restaurant, but when you get there, you find that the door is locked and there's a Closed sign. You look in the window and see a cook cleaning up, so you knock and ask him to make you something to eat. The cook refuses because the restaurant closed at ten. You think he's rude, and you get angry and insist that he help you. Then he starts to get angry too. You apologize and try to resolve the conflict. Fill in the chart with appropriate language.*

	Language for Expressing Anger	Language for Resolving Conflict
You		
The cook		

B. *Work with a partner. Take turns playing the roles in **A**, using the language for expressing anger and resolving conflict. Can you convince the cook to change his mind and make you something to eat?*

PRACTICE 7:
A Letter from Chicago

A. *Read each example. On the line, write **OK** if it's an acceptable sentence, **R** if it's a run-on sentence, **F** if it's a sentence fragment, or **NP** if it contains nonparallel constructions.*

_____ **1.** You wanted me to write about my first impressions of Chicago.

_____ **2.** Your prediction that I would find its busyness, noise, and filthy tiring has not happened.

_____ **3.** Before I arrived here, my imagination had conjured up amazing visions of this city, I had seen so many pictures of its famous buildings.

_____ **4.** My naive dream that skyscrapers would really scrape the sky.

_____ **5.** My first day here I couldn't wait to rush to the Sears Tower and peering up its many stories.

_____ **6.** The top was in sight, I could see it easily.

_____ **7.** The building wasn't as imposing as I had imagined, I was quite disappointed.

_____ **8.** Instead of taking the elevator to the top, I preferred to turn away and going walking in the park.

B. *Rewrite the sentences as a paragraph on a sheet of paper.*

The Sears Tower in Chicago

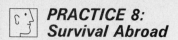 **PRACTICE 8:**
Survival Abroad

A. *Listen to the conversation and answer the questions.*

1. What problem is the company facing?

_____

2. Why do some people fail at jobs in cultures other than their own?

_____

3. What kinds of information would be helpful to an employee in coping
with a new culture?

_____

4. What kinds of information would be helpful to an employee's family
in adjusting to a new culture?

_____

5. What three negotiating styles are mentioned?

_____

_____

_____

B. *In what other situations would a course such as that described be
useful? List three or four.*

_____

_____

C. *If you were going to teach a course for foreign nationals coming to
study in your country, what would you include? List four or five
customs or attitudes you think these students would need to know
about.*

_____

_____

_____

D. *Work in a group. Your school often invites foreign professors to
teach classes. Unfortunately, a large majority leave before completing
their assignments. Many have indicated that the problem is not one of
academics but one of fitting in. You are a team that is trying to figure
out how to make these professors' experiences more positive so they
will stay until the end of the term. Discuss possible courses of action.
Be prepared to present your group's solutions to the class.*

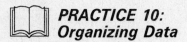

PRACTICE 9:
Hearing the Link

A. Listen to the sentence and write it on the line.

1. _____

2. _____

3. _____

4. _____

5. _____

B. Circle the words that have sound changes, additions, or deletions in each sentence. Some sentences may have more than one example.

C. Work with a partner. Take turns saying the sentences.

PRACTICE 10:
Organizing Data

A. Read the article and fill in the chart.

St. Petersburg

The history of the name of St. Petersburg reflects the changing political history of Russia itself. Before the reign of Peter the Great, czar from 1682 to 1723, Russia had little contact with the rest of the world. Peter traveled extensively through western Europe and became determined to open his country to the art and ideas he found there. Therefore, in 1703, he founded the city of St. Petersburg as a gateway to the Western world.

Peter brought artists and architects from all over Europe to build the city, which he named after his patron saint. In 1712, Peter moved the nation's capital from Moscow to St. Petersburg. Over the next two centuries, the city became the artistic and intellectual center of Russia, as well as a main industrial and engineering city.

After Russia went to war against Germany in 1914, at the start of World War I, the country's officials changed the name of St. Petersburg to Petrograd ("Peter's City" in Russian) to get rid of the German ending *burg*. It was in Petrograd that the Revolution of 1917, which ended czarist rule, broke out. Nikolai (Vladimir Ilyich) Lenin, founder of the Soviet government and its first premier, moved the capital back to Moscow in 1918. When he died in 1924, Petrograd was renamed Leningrad to honor him.

In the late 1980s the Communist party's tight control over the Soviet Union began to break up. In the 1990 elections, non-Communists won control of Leningrad's government. And in September, 1991, the name of Leningrad was changed back to St. Petersburg.

Year	Name of City	Reason for Name

B. What other device could be used to organize the information in the article? Draw another kind of chart on a sheet of paper.

PRACTICE 11:
A New Name

A. *A proposal has been made to change the name of your city to that of a famous citizen. Work with a partner and choose a citizen, living or dead, whom you think deserves the honor. Write some reasons why you think that person is worthy on a sheet of paper.*

B. *Form a group with your partner from* ***A*** *and two other pairs. You and your partner must try to convince the group to rename your city after the person of your choice. If a conflict arises, use compromise and concession to diffuse the tension and refocus the discussion. Take notes of the meeting.*

PRACTICE 12:
When in Rome

The Spanish Steps in Rome

A. *Read the concluding paragraph of an essay titled ''When in Rome, Do as the Romans Do.'' Then answer the questions.*

Therefore, no matter how much of a cliché you feel the expression ''When in Rome, do as the Romans do'' is, you should heed the advice. This is obviously true when visiting other countries, but it may also apply to visiting different parts of your own country, which may have different norms and expectations. In short, find out as much as you can about customs, etiquette, verbal and body language, and so on, before you leave, and keep this information in mind during your travels. If you respect people's culture, they will treat you well, and you will enjoy yourself more. Moreover, you may even learn something new about yourself.

1. From reading just the concluding paragraph, state the theme of the essay.

_____

2. From reading just the concluding paragraph, state one of the main ideas of the essay.

_____

3. What function do the last two sentences in the paragraph perform?

_____

B. *Use your notes from Practice 11 to write a short summary of your group's discussion on a sheet of paper. State the group's decision, explain the reasons for that city name, and provide a closure for your summary.*

Information for Practice 4: What Are You Referring To?

Stranger in a Strange Land, by Robert Heinlein, is the story of an earthling, born and educated on Mars, who visits planet Earth and views contemporary culture from an outsider's point of view.

In the song ''America the Beautiful,'' the lyricist, Katherine Lee Bates, praises her country by calling it ''beautiful for spacious skies, For amber waves of grain; For purple mountain majesties Above the fruited plain.''

A. Grammar

Rewrite the paragraphs on a sheet of paper. Correct all run-on sentences, sentence fragments, and nonparallel structures.

Nowadays many businesses must think about global issues when trying to market products, one example is a car with the name *Nova,* meaning "new" in the United States. It did not sell well in Latin America, where *no va* means "doesn't go."

Book covers too. They cannot always be the same in every country and cultural sensitivity must be taken into account. For example, using a drawing of people in swimsuits may be inappropriate in some countries or to show an incorrectly drawn Eiffel Tower would be insulting in France.

Tastes in design differ from country to country too. For example, designers in London feel that the covers of American books, both novels and nonfiction, are coarse because they do not use much illustration, instead they use big bold type and the colors are too garish. The American view is that British book covers are too weak, gentle, and have only a slight attractiveness.

B. Reading and Writing

You have just returned to your school after a semester of study abroad. You will get credit for the formal courses you took, but you feel you should get some credit for your life experiences as well. For example, you stayed in a very historic city and learned a lot about the history of the area. You learned to speak the dialect of the area very well too. The father of your host family was mayor of the town, so you found out how the government works. Write a letter to your counselor explaining why you think you should get history, language, and political science credits, along with any others you can think of and defend. When you are finished, file your letter in your writing portfolio.

PRACTICE 1:
Mentors

A. *As we get older, we may need not only role models, whom we admire from afar, but also mentors, from whom we can get advice and support in attaining our goals. Mentors can help their protégés in a variety of ways, for example, by helping them set priorities or by exposing them to new opportunities. Make an idea map.*

mentor

B. *Think about your own goals in life. What could a mentor do to help you achieve those goals? How could you go about finding a mentor? Share your ideas with the class.*

PRACTICE 2:
Networking

A. *One way to find a mentor is by networking—by developing a group of people and organizations from whom you can get professional and occupational advice. List three people or organizations you could go to for help in finding a mentor.*

_____

_____

_____

B. *List three specific things you would like a mentor to do for you. For example, you might like information about what it's like to work in a particular field or in a particular country.*

_____

_____

_____

C. *Network among your classmates. Find out if anyone in class has a friend or relative who can give you the help you listed in **B**.*

PRACTICE 3:
Using Prior Knowledge

A. Read the title of the article. What does it mean to have "second thoughts" about something? What ideas do you think the author will share about role models? List some ideas.

_____

_____

Second Thoughts About Role Models
by Dr. Johnnetta B. Cole

While it's important that our children learn about their country's heroes—and its "sheroes" (for "history" tends to overlook the great accomplishments of women)—it is also crucial for them to see role models in their everyday lives, to be motivated and inspired by extraordinary ordinary folks. When this happens, our children believe they too can become poets, physicists, or philosophers. They too can start shelters for the homeless, receive recognition as outstanding teachers, take the lead in organizing their communities against drugs. When our American heroes are portrayed as bigger than life—living, working, accomplishing beyond the realm of the normal—and when they are depicted as perfect human beings, incapable of succumbing to human frailty, they are placed so far from us that it seems impossible we could ever touch them or mirror who they are in our own lives. Elevating our heroes to the level of myth undermines their usefulness as role models. Our children don't need lessons in how to be superhuman. They need flesh-and-blood heroes and sheroes who can guide them in becoming the best human beings they can be. And we adults need role models too.

It is easy to write about heroes and sheroes—more difficult to consider myself one. There was a time when I did not want to be called a role model. It seemed to me that being a role model made life more demanding. A role model takes responsibility not only for her own life but also for some of the lives of others. A role model in the public eye is always "on." You think several times before wearing blue jeans to the grocery store. You must somehow make time for dozens of invitations to speak at the local women's club, church, or high school. It's no wonder I didn't want the job. I had bought in to the myth of the superhuman woman. I saw my human limitations as weaknesses. I've now come to understand that it is really all right to be another's role model, _especially_ if you have the ability to be human about it—to reach out and touch that young person, give her a hug when she needs it and a criticism when it's in order.

Being a role model doesn't mean not being yourself. It means being the best person you know how to be and being there for others. Each of us has that capability. Think of the heroes and sheroes in your life. None of them was perfect, but they made a difference, and so can you.

B. Dr. Cole, an anthropologist and educator, is president of Spelman College in Atlanta, Georgia. For whom do you think she acts as a role model? For whom might she act as a mentor? List your ideas.

_____

C. Why does Dr. Cole feel it's important to be a role model? For whom could you be a role model? How might being a role model or mentor benefit you? Share your ideas with a partner.

D. List the qualities Dr. Cole believes a role model should have.

_____

_____

PRACTICE 4:
Just Great!

A. English has many idioms signifying approval or disapproval. Read each example and write **A** for approval or **D** for disapproval.

_____ **1.** I didn't know how I had done on the test until she gave me the **thumbs up.** Then I knew I had passed.

_____ **2.** You're really insightful. You **hit the bull's-eye** yesterday when you said Jeannie would get the job.

_____ **3.** John is just **not my cup of tea.** I'm certainly not going to emulate him.

_____ **4.** Carl was happy to have Wong as a mentor; without him, Carl would never have **made the team.**

_____ **5.** I was really relieved after giving my speech. I knew I had done all right when my teacher gave me **a pat on the back.**

_____ **6.** I think Sarah **made a bad call** on that project. She'd better not do it again if she wants to keep her job.

_____ **7.** My grandfather has been very generous to me ever since I was a child. I guess I'm **the apple of his eye.**

_____ **8.** I never listen to their advice. It's usually **for the birds.**

B. Answer the questions.

1. Which of the idioms refer to animals? _____

2. Which of the idioms refer to sports? _____

3. Which of the idioms refer to food or drink? _____

4. Which of the idioms refer to body language? _____

C. Do you know idioms in your native language that are similar to these in meaning? that use similar images? Share your ideas with a partner.

PRACTICE 5:
It's Hard to Say Good-by

A. Choose one of the situations below and circle its number. List several examples of language for preclosing and closing a conversation for that situation.

1. A reunion of college professors and their student teaching assistants is ending.
2. The last English class of the year is almost over.
3. A teacher's convention is closing.
4. your own idea

Preclosing: _____

Closing: _____

B. Work as a group. Assign roles and act out the conversations your group members chose in **A.** Be sure everyone uses the correct level of formality.

PRACTICE 6:
Let's Agree

Circle the correct form of the verb in each sentence.

1. The Japanese **eat/eats** a lot of fish.

2. Japanese **is/are** an important language for international business.

3. Statistics **was/were** my hardest subject last year.

4. Statistics on the department's losses **is/are** not available.

5. Money **is/are** not the only goal of many business people.

6. The American people **is/are** almost all immigrants or the

   descendants of immigrants.

7. My new jeans **is/are** already wearing out.

8. No news **is/are** good news.

PRACTICE 7:
Who Was Your Mentor?

A. *Listen to the lecture and answer the questions.*

1. What is the speaker's profession?

_____

2. What is her definition of a mentor?

_____

3. Who were three of her mentors, and why did she admire each?

_____

_____

B. *Think about your own role models and/or mentors. List one reason you admire each one.*

Name	Relationship to You	Reason for Admiration

PRACTICE 8:
Shift for Yourself

A. *Listen to each pair of words. Underline the syllable that receives the strongest stress in each word.*

1. study   student
2. choreograph   choreography
3. geography   geographical
4. fragile   fragility
5. mobile   mobility
6. legal   legality
7. nation   national
8. national   nationality
9. grade   gradual
10. meter   metrical
11. decide   decision
12. pronounce   pronunciation
13. reduce   reduction
14. public   publicity
15. sign   signature

B. *Work with a partner. Take turns saying the pairs of words.*

PRACTICE 9:
Write It Out

These are the sources a student used to write a paper on mentors. Write the list of references on a sheet of paper. Use the style shown on page 146 of the Student Book. Remember to put the entries in alphabetical order.

Gail Sheehy/ New York/ 1974/ Passages: Predictable Crises in Adult Life/ E. P. Dutton and Company

Nancy W. Collins/ 1983/ Professional Women and Their Mentors: A Practical Guide to Mentoring/ Prentice-Hall/ Englewood Cliffs, NJ

Daniel J. Levinson/ "Growing Up with a Dream"/ pp. 20–34/ Psychology Today/ November 1978

T. Peters and R. Waterman, Jr./ Harper & Row/ 1982/ In Search of Excellence/ New York

K. Fury/ December 1979/ pp. 42–47/ Savvy/ "Mentor Mania"

A. Grammar

Circle the correct form of the verb in each sentence.

1. My family **is/are** planning a reunion in California this year.

2. Linguistics **is/are** my favorite subject.

3. Mumps **is/are** a very contagious disease.

4. **Do/Does** the police ever come to your school to discuss safety

   procedures?

5. The sheep **is/are** walking one behind the other.

6. The young **need/needs** encouragement to achieve their goals.

7. **Has/Have** your class improved since the beginning of the year?

8. The scissors **is/are** not sharp enough to cut this rope.

B. Reading/Writing

Usually a mentor and a protégé find each other by accident and team up because of mutual respect. Nowadays, however, many businesses, schools, and cities are setting up "mentoring programs." These programs assign older executives to younger ones, experienced teachers to those who are just starting their careers, or even business people to high-school students. These mentors give help and advice in both career and personal development. Write an essay explaining how such a program might be set up in your school or community. State the goals of the program and tell how you would persuade people to join. Explain how you would match the participants. When you are finished, file your essay in your writing portfolio.